HUNDRED PROOF

WILLIAM H. TOWNSEND

Hundred

Published by the

Proof

Salt River Sketches & Memoirs of the Bluegrass

Introduction by Holman Hamilton

UNIVERSITY OF KENTUCKY PRESS

Printed in the United States of America by the
University of Kentucky Printing Division
Library of Congress Catalog Card
No. 64-14002

To the memory of my father and mother
and to all the people of Glensboro and Anderson County
who made my boyhood such a happy experience

CONTENTS

ILLUSTRATIONS

INTRODUCTION

The Sage

OF ALL THE AMAZING storytellers in the colorful annals of the Bluegrass Commonwealth, a region famed for wit and humor, there is none like Bill Townsend. Born in Anderson County, Kentucky, on May 31, 1890, William Henry

of Salt River

Townsend grew up as the only child of a country doctor. The land of his youth is one associated with Lincoln kinsmen, Confederate veterans, and twentieth-century leaders like Champ Clark. Townsend's boyhood was spent in the Salt River Valley, ten miles from the county seat of Lawrenceburg—his home being the doctor's frame cottage in a village known as Camdenville or Orr, which became Glensboro in 1904. He was educated in one-room schoolhouses, took "advanced" courses from a Transylvania College master of arts, and then entered Kentucky Agricultural and Mechanical College which later grew into the University of Kentucky.

The Anderson County of Bill Townsend's youth was a relaxed and rural place, far removed from the burgeoning industrialism of a changing nation. It was true that the city of Louisville, where Bill's father had obtained his medical education, was only sixty-five miles from Lawrenceburg, and a traveler could board a Southern Railway train for the two-and-a-half-hour westward excursion to the state's metropolis. Lexington, thirty-four miles east of Glensboro, could be reached on a branch line of the Southern from Lawrenceburg. And a visit to the state capital of Frankfort, in a county adjoining Anderson, involved a horse-and-buggy trip of an hour and three-quarters over a rough, crooked, and very narrow road. Lexington and Frankfort had been places of size and importance when Chicago and Milwaukee were clusters of cabins, but when Bill was five, and ten, and fifteen years old, the growth of these Kentucky communities was slow. The life of their people, in the main, was leisurely. And throughout Central Kentucky there was much of the same mingling of frontier earthiness and Virginia-oriented gentility which earlier marked Kentucky generations of the antebellum days.

The blend of the earthy and the genteel has characterized Bill Townsend all his life. In great measure it is traceable to the influence of his father, Oliver L. Townsend. A native of McLean County who was graduated at the head of his class at the old Hospital College of Medicine in Louisville, the father represented all that is meaningful in that nostalgic term "the country doctor." In every kind of weather and at any hour of night or day the physician might be encountered somewhere in the county—his side-bar buggy bumping along rutted roads or dragging painfully through the mire behind the big bay mare "Topsy" as its driver sought to hurry on to tend an ailing older patient or to preside at a baby's birth.

Almost equally familiar to residents of "Old Anderson," especially when school was out, was the sight of the doctor's little son occupying the seat beside him as he went on his round of calls. In the father-son companionship many of Bill Townsend's most memorable qualities had their origin and nurture. The two discussed all sorts of things, from farmers' toil and neighbors' quirks to politics and literature. Dr. Townsend had a keen eye for personality and character and a taste for reading. He especially liked the novels of Charles Dickens, the poetry of Tennyson and Bryant, and the editorials of "Marse Henry" Watterson in the Louisville *Courier-Journal.*

Young Townsend's mother, nee Susan Mary Brown, was also an important influence in his boyhood and adolescence. A resident of Camdenville at the time of her marriage to the physician in 1882, she was the granddaughter of a pioneer settler of Anderson County. One of the aspects of her early life which always impressed her son was that she had been a pupil of Champ Clark—then far from the Speakership of the United States House of Representatives—when he taught in Camdenville's village school. William H. Townsend, who attended the same school, was (as he likes to say) "unevenly educated." When the time came to enter Kentucky A. & M., he could not get into the freshman class in mathematics but by examination was qualified for and did enter the junior class in history. His interest in words and phrases started early. At his father's suggestion, beginning when Bill was about ten years old the boy would look up the definitions of six or seven words daily and then talk to his parents about them. As an Anderson County youngster he was fortunate in having as a teacher Ezra L Gillis, a stanch friend and later Registrar of the University of Kentucky. Another teacher who made a special impression on him was William Case, the Transylvania alumnus. "A dreamy fella," Townsend remembered, "who had a singularly melodious voice." Case inculcated in the youthful Townsend more love and appreciation of English and American literature than any other person at any stage of his life.

While the lads in William Case's class practiced their penmanship, the mentor liked to read to them from Poe, Irving, and the British poets. One of the oft-repeated passages was that of Alexander Pope, beginning:

> Lo, the poor Indian! whose untutor'd mind
> Sees God in clouds, or hears him in the wind.

The day came when a schoolmate of Townsend's raised a hand and addressed the master.

"Tell us more about Lo," the boys requested.

Case was puzzled. "Who?" he asked.

"Lo," the pupil repeated.

"Who is Lo?"

"Why, 'Lo, the poor Indian'—the one you read us about before," the boy explained.

That is one of the minor-key Townsend tales, used by the Kentucky raconteur to evoke chuckles from his friends and put them in a mood for more hilarious yarns. From his Anderson County years many another story has come—the sabre-rattling of the Bridge Hill "Hant," the account of the secret weapon hidden in the one-armed man's long sleeve, and other equally colorful anecdotes reproduced on following pages. There is much about present-day Glensboro (no bigger than it was in 1904) and the Salt River and its valley that seems peculiarly appropriate to Bill Townsend. The yarn spinner "belongs" with the farmers and village people of the area. Although he has been associated with Lexington for over half a century, the customs and traditions, the pathos and humor, of the banks of Salt River cling to him.

The Kentucky Agricultural and Mechanical College, or "State College" as it usually was called, was just coming into its own in the first decade of the twentieth century. Up to that time denominational colleges—first Transylvania, and then Danville's Centre College—had set the pace for Kentucky's institutions of higher learning. The "State College" that is now the University of Kentucky had its inception as early as 1862, in the Morrill Land Grant College Law. Its advancement was tardy, however, and not until around Bill Townsend's time did it become rather widely recognized for its cultural courses as well as for the classes in agriculture and related subjects. Located in ever-charming Lexington, it was presided over by James K. Patterson, a crippled Scotsman nicknamed "He Pat" (to distinguish him from a brother known as "She Pat") by irreverent underclassmen.

In some of these pages Bill recalls quaint episodes of his college days. He tells of "starting" his freshman year three times before he could overcome the onslaughts of homesickness, and about the transformation of He Pat's gray horse, "Old Rollo," into a reasonable facsimile of a zebra. He does not include very much about certain other aspects of campus life, such as his membership in the Delta Chi fraternity, service as editor-in-chief of the college newspaper, or the work he did and the fun he had in helping to edit the yearbook. As would be expected by anyone who later knew the mature Bill Townsend, he excelled in public speaking as an undergraduate. In his sophomore year he won the much coveted Crum Oratorical Medal over six contestants—five seniors and one junior. James H. Mulligan, who wrote the famous poem "In Kentucky," was one of the judges. In the spring of 1910, when he was just turning twenty, he was a member of the State College varsity debating team that defeated Georgetown College in Lexington, taking the negative side of the woman suffrage question. The following year, as president of the Kentucky Intercollegiate Debating Association, Bill acted as chairman and wielded the gavel when Georgetown and Centre were forensic rivals and State College and Transylvania were opponents. Thus, in connection with both the written and the spoken word, young Townsend excelled in the eyes of his student contemporaries.

When Bill went to Lexington for his third, and this time successful, try at being a freshman, he planned to take a premedical course and eventually to enter his father's profession. For various reasons he changed his mind. One was his trips to the Fayette County Courthouse, where he was enthralled by the attorneys whom he saw and heard there. While he continued taking many liberal arts subjects, the law increasingly appealed to him and he received the LL.B. degree in 1912 without ever obtaining the arts degree. Bill's legal studies were valuable in another way, by no means incidental. It was no accident that while a Law School senior he was made "legal adviser" of the Alpha Gamma Delta sorority—"a very pleasant undertaking," as he remembers. One of the Alpha Gam pledges in the fall of 1911 was an attractive young lady named Genevieve Johnson, daughter of Benjamin Franklin Johnson and Mary Dillon Johnson of Linneus, Linn County, Missouri. Miss Johnson was graduated from State College in early June of 1915, and on the sixteenth of that month she became Mrs. William H. Townsend. The honeymoon was in Chicago.

In a very real sense it has been a honeymoon ever since. No man ever had a more devoted wife than the Bluegrass lawyer, and early in their married life he had occasion to show his own devotion. Not long after the birth of the Townsends' only child, Mary Genevieve, the young mother fell ill with typhoid fever; her recovery was not as rapid as desired, which gave the Lexington family doctor and several specialists much concern. It was thought advisable for Mrs. Townsend to go to Asheville, North Carolina, for a rest cure—and there she did considerably better under medical supervision in a cottage on a mountainside overlooking the Grove Park Inn. While her mother and baby were with her, Bill's visits provided high points of her months of recuperation. Her husband was doing well professionally, being associated with the celebrated Richard C. Stoll in the Lexington firm of Stoll & Bush since graduation. "Did you practice criminal law?" Bill recently was asked. "Criminal and civil and uncivil," he replied. "Everything was fish that came to the net." From Thanksgiving of 1918 until the next September, however, Judge Stoll's junior partner absented himself as frequently as possible from law books and courtrooms, taking the midnight train at Lexington—often on Fridays—and customarily reaching Asheville at half-past one the following afternoon.

It might be supposed that dedication to the law would lead Bill Townsend to admire a lawyer, Kentuckian by birth, who became a world figure as well as President of the United States—Abraham Lincoln. Perhaps that had something to do with the ultimate depth and breadth of his studies. But in 1919 the future collector, author, and authority on the Sixteenth President formed a nodding acquaintance with Lincoln quite by accident in the course of one of his Carolina visits. Strolling into a second-hand bookstore in Asheville, Townsend browsed a bit and then paid a dollar for his first Lincoln book. It was *The Portrait Life of Abraham*

Lincoln, by Francis Trevelyan Miller, which is still in his library. New vistas unrolled as he perused the volume. Soon he was purchasing other Lincoln works, many of which cost many times the price of *The Portrait Life.*

One of Townsend's relatively early acquisitions was *The Paternity of Abraham Lincoln* by William E. Barton. An eminent Congregationalist minister in Oak Park, Illinois, Dr. Barton soon found in his mail the Townsend copy of the book with a request that it be inscribed by the author. This led to Barton's asking Townsend to check Kentucky deeds, mortgages, and related records concerning the Sparrow family—Lucy Hanks (Lincoln's maternal grandmother) having married Henry Sparrow when Nancy Hanks was a child. The research performed on Barton's behalf proved a natural and congenial entree into the sphere of Lincoln scholarship. Not only did Bill Townsend uncover much documentary material, but when Dr. Barton visited Central Kentucky, Townsend introduced the clergyman to many of Lucy Hanks Sparrow's descendants, a number of whom had been patients of his father in Anderson County. Increasingly intimate association with Barton brought Bill into the inner circle of Lincoln students, and the minister dedicated his *The Lineage of Lincoln* "to my friend, William H. Townsend, who has traveled with me over thousands of the miles that made this book possible and who knows the labor, adventures, disappointments and occasional rejoicings which our pilgrimages extending over many years have brought."

The Barton-Townsend friendship grew so close that, when Barton became ill in 1930 in the midst of his work on *President Lincoln,* he asked the attorney to finish the book "should I fall by the wayside." Barton died in December, 1930, and Townsend in due course fulfilled his promise, completing the volume and writing the preface. On February 12, 1933, the New York *Times'* critic commented: "Mr. Townsend has himself made important contributions to the Lincoln bibliography, and his present chapters have a literary distinction which calls for special praise."

The *Times* reviewer was alluding to other Lincoln studies which Townsend had undertaken during the decade of the 1920s. The first of these was *Abraham Lincoln, Defendant,* published by the Houghton Mifflin Company of Boston in 1922. Then came *Lincoln the Litigant* (1925), likewise bearing the Houghton Mifflin imprint. The volume which did most to establish Townsend's reputation as an authority was *Lincoln and His Wife's Home Town,* a charming account of Abraham and Mary Todd Lincoln and the Lexington of the Civil War and antebellum periods which contained fresh material and was brought out in Indianapolis by the Bobbs-Merrill Company in 1929. *Lincoln and Liquor* followed in 1934, and *Lincoln and the Bluegrass* (a very well received and handsomely illustrated major work of the University of Kentucky Press) in 1955. While he invariably treats his native region with unalloyed affection and Lincoln with sympathy and admiration, Townsend yet manages to attain no small measure of objectivity and perspective. As one commentator pointed out, "Mr. Townsend's kinsmen during the Civil War were on the Southern side, many of them in the Confederate Army; but he writes with fearlessly clearsighted impartiality, holding the subject aloft as a jewel of complicated cut, searching keenly its many angles, revealing surprising things, some ugly, some beautiful."

There is no doubt in the minds of his friends that Bill Townsend would have written many more books if he had not been so busy a member of the Fayette County Bar. One of Lexington's leading attorneys, he practiced throughout the state and represented clients who had cases before the United States Supreme Court. He served as Chief Corporation Counsel of Lexington for twelve years, from 1920 to 1932, and has won the confidence of many corporate and individual clients. He also took part in local politics and was Augustus Owsley Stanley's Fayette County chairman in his campaigns for the United States Senatorship and the Governorship of Kentucky. Townsend received the honorary degree of Doctor of Laws from the University of Kentucky in 1930, and the honorary Doctorate of Literature from Lincoln Memorial University in 1946. After his term as national president of the University of Kentucky Alumni Association, he was made an honorary life member of the association's Executive Committee. Noteworthy honors have included election to Omicron Delta Kappa, to Phi Alpha Theta, and to Phi Beta Kappa. He was one of the twelve appointees of President Eisenhower to the National Lincoln Sesquicentennial Commission, was chairman of the Kentucky Lincoln Sesquicentennial Commission, and vice chairman of the Kentucky Civil War Centennial Commission. Lincoln groups and Civil War Round Tables from New York to southern California have made him an honorary member.

Historians, newspapermen, magazine writers, college presidents, and other nationally known visitors to Lexington have been impressed by members of a small and informal gathering of kindred spirits who called themselves the "Book Thieves." Originating almost haphazardly in the latter part of the 1920s, this organization (if such it may be called) was composed of a few men who enjoyed each other's company and shared an appreciation of cultural themes and of Kentuckiana in general. In this group Bill Townsend was drawn to J. Winston Coleman, Jr., tobacco farmer and author of *Slavery Times in Kentucky* and other significant books; by the time the Coleman-Townsend friendship was well developed, Coleman was busily engaged in assembling the largest and finest of all collections of Kentucky books. Another cherished friend was then a younger member of the Book Thieves, Dr. Thomas D. Clark, chairman of the University of Kentucky's Department of History and a gifted and productive scholar.

One of the older "breth-er-en" (as Townsend pronounces the word) in the charmed circle was the then President of the University of Kentucky, Dr. Frank L. McVey. And when Dr. Herman L. Donovan succeeded McVey and moved to Lexington from Richmond, Kentucky, he was invited to join those who held forth in "the feast of reason and the flow of soul." Judge Samuel M. Wilson, whose collection of rare Kentuckiana is now in the University of Kentucky Library, was also an ardent member of this group. Meetings, held at various members' houses, started with luncheon on Saturday noon and went on through the afternoon with Townsend's quips, anecdotes, and sallies among the highlights of the repartee. When his turn came to play host to his friends, they were welcomed to the house at 28 Mentelle Park which he had bought soon after his marriage—and subsequently to "Helm Place," the columned mansion on the Bowman Mill Road which he purchased in 1946.

Townsend's friendship for "Squire" Coleman inspired some lines, described by the lawyer-historian as his "first and only venture into verse." In 1942 the

Townsends traveled out to the Pacific Coast for the wedding of Mrs. Townsend's niece at Santa Barbara, California. On the way west, they visited Arizona. Sitting near the rim of the Grand Canyon, Bill was not unaware of the grandeur of the scene before him. But at the same time his strong sensibility, acute awareness of the absence of valued associates, and homesickness for a distant Kentucky all came into play. And so he dashed off "The Squire":

> If one would know real Bluegrass charm,
> He first must stop at Winburn Farm
> And meet the Squire.
> Nobody here is ever bored.
> Gray shadows dance on Morgan's sword
> Above the fire.
>
> The Squire leans back among his books,
> The pioneer stalks from leafy nooks
> With his powder horn.
> "Let's talk of Boone and Clark," he'll say,
> "Zac Taylor, too, at Monterey,
> And sip our corn."

These verses not only summarize Townsend's warm regard for a special friend but also demonstrate the rare mingling of culture and humanity epitomized in his mind by a fellow Book Thief and by a favorite Book Thieves' rendezvous.

Identification with Helm Place has also meant a great deal to Bill Townsend. When Bill settled in Lexington, the owner was Mrs. Emilie Todd Helm, who was Mrs. Lincoln's half sister and the widow of Confederate General Ben Hardin Helm, who died at Chickamauga. The house is one of the most appealing antebellum edifices in the Bluegrass; its wide hall, high ceilings, winding stairway, and well-executed portraits have proved attractive to several generations of guests. Townsend became a friend of Mrs. Helm and of her children—Miss Katherine Helm, Mrs. Waller Lewis, and Ben Hardin Helm, Jr. He greatly admired Miss Katherine's portrait of Mrs. Lincoln, which she herself painted and which hangs in one of the parlors at Helm Place today. She also made a copy of this portrait which today hangs in the White House. Another bond was the help he gave her in gathering information for her book on the wartime First Lady, entitled *Mary, Wife of Lincoln.* Mr. and Mrs. Joe Murphy, son-in-law and daughter of the Townsends, now reside at Helm Place with their daughter Mary Elodie. The Townsends spend weekends there or drive out for Sunday dinner. In and near the guest house there are said to be French-speaking ghosts—descendants, says Bill, of a Morocco boy whom the Marquis de Lafayette brought with him from France in 1825 and who fell in love with a mulatto girl owned by the first squire of Helm Place, Colonel Abraham Bowman, who served under Lafayette during the Revolution.

Numerous Lincoln and Civil War authorities cherish memories of hours and days when they joined Bill Townsend in enjoying his favorite Fayette County sights. Any list of the authors and scholars he has known well should include Allan Nevins of Columbia University and the Huntington Library; Bruce Catton, editor of *American Heritage;* R. Gerald McMurtry, director of the Lincoln National Life Foundation; Bell I. Wiley of Emory University; T. Harry Williams of Louisiana State University; Edgar DeWitt Jones, author of *Lords of Speech* and *Lincoln and the Preachers,* a distinguished Detroit minister of the Christian Church; Albert J. Beveridge, who wrote biographies of John Marshall and Abraham Lincoln after representing Indiana in the Senate; and then of course Carl Sandburg.

Excerpts of letters from Sandburg convey the quality and nature of the Townsend personality as thoroughly as any documents can. In 1935, from West Virginia, the famous poet-biographer wrote:

> Brudder Townsend
>
> Your pint of Ky Tavern is not half finished as yet but I will remember you long after it is gone. That was a grand afternoon of talk, many fragments of it sticking close with me now. Good going to you—
>
> As always
>
> CARL SANDBURG.

Then there are the two communications dated 1959. "Our fellowship has lasted well across the years," Sandburg wrote from North Carolina in January of that year. "I hope sometime to again get to Lexington and walk around with you looking at sculpture [*i.e.*, the equestrian statue of John Hunt Morgan—see Chapter 14] and much else—and listening to a voice that recorded a marvelous portrait of one of the most vivid characters that ever came out of Kentucky [Cassius M. Clay (1810-1903)]. About twice a year I listen to this. You have terrific finality in so pleasing and casual a voice. . . . You have roots going deep in the Lincoln personality and tradition. Ever loving regard to you." And the following July: "There are many dear Bills and only one dear Bill Townsend. 'When God made him he broke the mold.' . . . The warmth of you, your capacity for fellowship, your original and exclusive contribution in the Lincoln field, these are deep in the hearts and minds of probably more good people than you are aware of."

The Cassius Marcellus ("Cash") Clay to whom Sandburg was referring was the fiery emancipationist, orator, bowie-knife wielder, and Minister to Russia, about whom Townsend delivered his most memorable speech without notes or manuscript. The date was October 17, 1952, and members of the Chicago Civil War Round Table were the original auditors. But the remarks were taped and records made, so that thousands of persons who never knew or saw the speaker have shared in the enjoyment. An abbreviated version of the address, containing many of its most pungent phrases, appears hereafter between these boards. Joe Creason of the Louisville *Courier-Journal* has said of it: "The speech is a classic, covering in dramatic fashion the career of Clay and done in all the detail and humor which is a Townsend trademark." Don Whitehead of the Associated Press concurred: "Townsend's speech is certain to become an American epic. I salute the gentleman from Kentucky whose drawling wit and pathos bring history alive so that you can see it, feel it, and smell it. Any man who can do that is a great orator."

Bill received many letters just after the delivery of this speech. Lester O. Schriver, now executive vice president of the National Association of Life Underwriters and one of the founders of the Chicago Round Table, who is himself a noted afterdinner speaker and Lincoln scholar, wrote in part: "As long as I live, I shall never forget the evening we spent with you at the Civil War Round Table Meeting. You were at your characteristic and inimitable best. The ovation which you received must have warmed your heart. It was one of the most spontaneous and affectionate I have ever witnessed and I couldn't keep the tears out of my eyes. Honestly, Bill, I was thrilled to the very limit of my capacity. You were eloquent, you were warm and friendly and your satire is unsurpassed by any man I have ever seen. I am just trying to tell you, you are Bill Townsend which is a manner of man that never has and never can be duplicated—and I am glad."

It seems probable that when a book-length study is made of the Townsend style and the Townsend "techniques," the analyst will conclude that something deeper than mere technique must be sought to explain the success of Bill Townsend as a writer and as a speaker. Then it may be determined that part of the explanation lies in the degree to which he has immersed himself in topics on which he chooses to hold forth, whether in oral remarks or in writing. It is no accident, for example, that a man who has written so knowledgeably about President Lincoln is a major collector of Lincolniana. Law books of the Lincoln & Herndon firm, the very copy of the first book on law which Lincoln studied, some of the choicest original Lincoln letters, meaningful items of nearly every sort associated with Lincoln—these are but a few of the contents of the magnificent Lincoln collection, inaugurated with the Miller volume in 1919 and steadily expanded through the years.

Lincoln broadsides, statuettes, daguerreotypes, engravings, and even the President's watch and chain gradually joined the Townsend treasure trove. Moreover (and this is particularly important), it was not as a hoarder—not as one who acquired historical objects simply for the sake of acquiring—but as a re-creator of Lincoln the man and Lincoln the statesman that the lawyer-author-orator pursued what became more significant than any casual hobby. For, at least as much as any other scholar I have known, Bill Townsend the speaker and Bill Townsend the author will invariably be found to have both a passion for detail and a loving regard for what details signify. Thus every ingredient of his Lincoln collection has made its way into the Townsend personality and the Townsend literary and oratorical gems as well as into whatever catalogue he has chosen to make of his possessions. In another field of interest, Townsend has in a sense "collected" Cassius Marcellus Clay the man while acquiring Clay's bowie knives, and papers, and books concerning Clay's bizarre life. And the salty son of Anderson County has "collected" Anderson County in the same sense—and Salt River, and State College, and Lexington, and Fayette County, and the Commonwealth, and the Civil War. These are part of the scholar-collector, and he "belongs" to them even as they "belong" to him.

In recent years several hundred fellow Kentuckians have welcomed the opportunity to make periodic contact with Bill Townsend through the Kentucky Civil War Round Table. At Round Table meetings—held on the third Monday evenings of September, November, January, March, and May—they have relished the Townsend comradeship and the Townsend rhetoric.

Bill has been president of the Round Table, reelected over and over again, ever since its inception in the autumn of 1953. His warm friend, Dr. Hambleton Tapp, has been secretary of the organization throughout. The Townsend-Tapp combination has proved so successful that repeatedly local guests and out-of-town visitors comment that they never knew or heard of any comparable group with similar spirit anywhere in the United States. Invited speakers, carefully screened, have been the best. Numerous winners of Pulitzer Prizes and other awards have aroused the enthusiasm of the dinner gatherings and helped to swell the Round Table membership from small beginnings to well over three hundred. But, without underestimating the eloquence and factual mastery of scholars from afar, the real tone is set time after time by Townsend's own contributions while presiding.

Again and again men like Dr. Donovan, Dr. Tapp, Dr. Edward H. Ray, Laurie J. Blakely, Edward S. Dabney, Fred B. Wachs, and Rhea A. Taylor have exclaimed after Round Table meetings: "What a shame it is that Bill's tall tales and whimsical thrusts, and especially the turns of phrase which are his own trademarks and characteristics, have not been captured in type for the joy of history lovers and humor lovers everywhere!" So it is that, in this container, the essence of Townsendiana—"Old Townsend" if you please—has been bottled. Here ripe wisdom, specialized scholarship, and a fine feeling for human splendor and human frailty have been distilled in unique proportions. Here we find the Kentucky flavor—and the rich, warm, rewarding fellowship of a great soul and a great friend.

Lexington, Kentucky
September 1963.

HOLMAN HAMILTON

HUNDRED PROOF

CHAPTER ONE

Glensboro

GLENSBORO, quiet village of fond memories, nestles dreamily in the lush bottom lands of the Salt River Valley ten miles west of Lawrenceburg, Kentucky.

Some years before the middle of the last century, Elijah Orr was quick to see the power possibilities of

and Ole Bill

the river bed's considerable decline from a point just east of what we boys called the "Cat Hole," and he built his grist mill with its huge undershot wheel at the end of a millrace nearly a mile long. About this time Tom Montgomery erected a carding factory—where wool was processed for spinning—and also a log still-house, which, with additions, later became known as the John E. Day Distillery.

These were the first industries in the community that soon became known as "Camden" or "Camdenville," although the name of the postoffice during most of my boyhood and for a long time previous was "Orr." I had always supposed that "Camden" or "Camdenville" were terms of mere local usage until I discovered an official list of postoffices in the United States and Territories for 1860-1861, which designates for Anderson County the following: "Camdenville, Chesher's Store (now Fox Creek), Johnsonville, Lawrenceburgh, Rough and Ready (now Alton), and Van Buren."

The people of the village detested "Orr" as the name of the Camden postoffice. When they went anywhere and said they were from "Orr," some wag was always ready with the wisecrack query: "Or what?" So in 1904 my father, O. L. Townsend, the country doctor, W. L. Franklin, and T. W. Calvert, merchants, and others decided to do their utmost to change the name of the postoffice and of the village itself.

Alton B. Parker was then the Democratic candidate for President against Teddy Roosevelt and, since most of the voters in the community were of Parker's political faith, there was, in the beginning, strong sentiment for "Parkersburg" or "Parkersville." Realizing that Washington authorities were stubborn about making such a change, especially if it involved a name of long standing, the committee enlisted the aid of the village's famous son, Champ Clark, who had spent his youth and young manhood in the fine old dwelling where Joe Sparrow now lives and had taught in the original schoolhouse near the bridge.

Clark, a Congressman from Missouri, later became Speaker of the House of Representatives and in 1912 narrowly lost the Democratic presidential nomination to Woodrow Wilson. Champ promptly conferred with the Post Office Department and reported that he had been reminded that "Parkersburg" was the name of an important town in West Virginia and that there were other towns in the various states named "Parkersville"; therefore, the Department did not look with favor on the names submitted. Someone then suggested that since the village was located in a valley or glen the name of "Glensboro" would be appropriate. Clark thought the officials would go along with this proposal.

Glensboro was a thriving place when I was growing up, especially on Saturday afternoons when people up and down the valley and across the hills came to mill and to do their trading. When I can first remember, the village had a busy mill, powered by both steam and water, two large stores and a smaller one, a distillery, a cooper shop, a new schoolhouse, two churches, a carding factory, a blacksmith shop, and a jail or "lock-up"—a small one-room affair just back of the blacksmith's shop, with walls of double rows of two-by-fours bolted together. Inside was a tiny, rusty stove, a battered coal bucket, a small beat-up lard can with a top on it, a stool, and an old shuck mattress on a low, rickety platform. The heavy oak door was reinforced by strips of thick plank, studded with rivets and two iron bars. During all the years I lived in Glensboro, I never knew of anybody being committed to this bastille nor did I hear that anybody had ever been so confined, except "Ole Bill," the village drunkard—and this was only for the purpose of sobering him up.

"Ole Bill" was a character who deserves to be put in a book. He was from a poor but well respected family. His great-great-grandfather, whose full name he bore, was a Revolutionary soldier. His grandfather —also having the same full name—marched away to war in Mexico with the boys recruited largely from the Valley who are still referred to in battle annals as the "fierce and indomitable Salt River Tigers," but he did not live to come back with them.

When I first saw Ole Bill he had lost his right arm just above the elbow, and he had a long knife scar stretching from his left ear to his mouth. Though illiterate, he had a high degree of natural intelligence. He was a good worker when sober: an "odd-jobs" man—washing buggies, cleaning stables and harness, killing hogs, whitewashing fences, raking leaves in the fall, and cleaning up yards in springtime. No employer ever denied that Bill gave him a full day's work.

Psychiatrists would doubtless lay the cause of Ole Bill's drinking to frustration or to a feeling of inferiority, but he would have scorned these new-fangled notions.

He was utterly free from all such complexes. His reason for drinking whiskey was simple and reasonable enough, at least to him—he liked it! Certainly he did not feel inferior because the whole village chuckled when, on one occasion—sublimely disregarding the trivialities of contradiction—Ole Bill expressed the opinion that "one man was as good as another and a durn sight better!"

I shall never forget the warm, moonlit night, shortly after the close of the Spanish-American War, when two young veterans of that short and not very bloody conflict, on their way home to Spencer County, alighted from their buggy and walked into Franklin's Store. Carefree and with pockets full of mustering-out pay, each had, as George Washington once wrote about his gardener Philip Bates, "suffered himself to be disguised with liquor." They bought some cigars and made a few other purchases; but they also, repeatedly and loudly, spouted the few Spanish words they had picked up in Cuba, boasted of their military exploits, kicked over a cracker barrel, and made themselves generally obnoxious.

Presently Ole Bill came in. He was also somewhat "disguised," having just consumed a formidable slug of the distillery's "singlings" or "first shots." Immediately the two veterans began making critical remarks about Bill's unkempt appearance, his one arm, and the livid scar on his face, asking him what war *he* had been in. Silently Bill turned around and left the store.

A short time later someone came running down the

pike to the doctor's little cottage at the foot of the hill shouting that he had just discovered two men, apparently dead, near the side of Franklin's Store. When the doctor hurriedly arrived on the scene he found the two individuals who had so valiantly served their country lying side by side, as cold and inert as two sticks of cordwood. Although it was about closing time Mr. Franklin had them carried into the store where, with some work on the part of the doctor, the men finally came to and sat up, rubbing their heads.

What had happened? They did not know! All they could say was that, when they came out of the store to get into their buggy, Ole Bill was waiting for them. He seemed quietly but deeply incensed at the remarks they had made about him. He said that while he had never been in a war he had seen some fighting in his time—something he doubted they had ever seen—and had followed this observation by declaring that, crippled though he was, he could whip both of them put together. When they rushed him he had feinted with his left and then swung the long sleeve which covered the stump of his right arm. Seeing nothing of a menacing nature about this, they had not bothered to duck, and in the next instant consciousness had completely deserted them!

Later on, when inquiry was made of Ole Bill, he quickly cleared up the mystery. He said he realized that in an encounter with these ex-soldiers who had insulted him without cause, he was at a distinct disadvantage—one hand against four. Hence, when he left the store, he had picked up a rock somewhat smaller than a tennis ball, unbuttoned his coarse, heavy shirt, and slipped the missile down his right sleeve, the end of which was stoutly stitched. The result? A blackjack, all the more deadly because its true nature was entirely concealed! Never again in street fights did any adversary ignore the possibility of grave danger from this crude but terribly efficient weapon.

Ole Bill lived in obscurity and endured, with outward indifference, the stigma invariably attached to a town drunkard. Probably no one now living knows when he died or where he is buried. Doubtless he lies in an unmarked grave. However, I think it is only right to point out that, though his fault was grievous, he harmed nobody but himself, and with it all he had certain sterling qualities that many of those who ridiculed him never possessed. He was honest; he was truthful; he was warm-hearted. Though having no family of his own, he was especially kind and helpful to widows and their broods of fatherless children and to others in sorrow and distress.

I simply cannot believe that the Angel, writing in the Book of Life, took none of this into account. In fact, if I am ever so fortunate as to be allowed to enter the Pearly Gates, I shall not be at all surprised to meet Ole Bill strolling serenely along the Golden Cobblestones, a large, eighteen-carat pebble in the end of his empty sleeve!

CHAPTER TWO

The Bridge

GHOSTS—spooks—"hants" were frequent topics of childish conversation around Glensboro firesides during long winter evenings. These sessions always produced wonderful goose-pimples and spine-tinglings; but they were hard on the small visitors who had to start home at bedtime. I remember fre-

Hill "Hant"

quently running breathlessly along the dark streets all the way to our little cottage, glancing apprehensively over my shoulder at almost every step. And when I stumbled and fell, as I sometimes did, the spook seemed right on top of me!

Bud Oliver had been in his grave many a year, but

folks who lived in a certain house in the village still pointed to reddish-brown splotches on the floor of the living room where Bud's bloody head had rested for a short time after he was shot. "Uncle" Hiram Busey and his wife "Aunt" Mary, former slaves and the only colored people in the village or anywhere else closer than Lawrenceburg, vowed that now and then—usually in the "thud quata ob de moon"—they had seen "Mista Bud," gun on shoulder, walking up and down in the yard near the well where Bob Mosely had killed him.

One Saturday I had been riding with my father all day. We had gone over some problems in simple arithmetic which I was preparing for Monday, as my father patiently realized that mathematics would always be the one dark cloud in the otherwise sunlit skies of all my school days. He remembered how perfectly outraged I had been when first confronted with that devil's invention—the multiplication table! We were almost home when a messenger galloped around a bend in the road and informed the doctor that an elderly farmer who lived some distance up Timber Creek suddenly had become violently ill. It was dark when we got there. My father hitched his horse to a tree at the foot of the hill some little distance from the house, and thinking that the patient might have some communicable disease he suggested that I remain in the buggy, saying he did not believe he would be gone long.

The moon was rising over the nearby woods and a sharp, gusty wind was blowing up, throwing scudding clouds across the sky. Suddenly I remembered hearing a man at the blacksmith shop only a short time before say that the sick farmer, who recently had lost his wife, had told him he believed her spirit still lingered about the old home. He said that on several occasions when he came in from work his wife's empty chair had been rocking back and forth and that one time as he approached the house he had heard her singing!

Well, this disquieted me no end, and I could not stay in the buggy any longer. I got out and began walking up and down near the gate where the footpath went up the hill to the house. Then, through the trees and underbrush across the creek, quite a little distance away, I saw something tall and white in the dim moonlight. As I gazed at it the "thing" seemed to raise a long, bleached arm and beckon in my direction! I was not mistaken about this—even in my jittery state of mind—because, in a few moments, *it did it again!*

It was lucky for me that about this time my father came down the path. I told him what the situation was and pointed out the "thing" that had waved at me so menacingly. He thought my eyes had deceived me. He said he knew what it was, and it couldn't possibly move. However, in order to convince me he suggested that we go up there and see for ourselves. So we crossed the creek, pushed through some heavy undergrowth along a steep bluff, and found a short, narrow tobacco bed with canvas loosely stretched over hickory wickets to keep it off the young plants. But the "thing" did move, even as we watched! A gust of wind caught one of the corners, flung the canvas off the wickets into the air, and dropped it back on the bed again.

"My son," said my father, "always remember this. If you see anything you can't explain, don't run away; find out what it is. This will clear up all mystery. I've traveled this country night and day for almost thirty years, and I've followed this rule to good advantage."

One of the tragic incidents of the Civil War resulted in an amusing tale about the Bridge Hill "Hant." On July 12, 1862, a bloody skirmish occurred at Camden between Lieutenant Tom Allen's Confederates and a detachment of Union cavalry and mounted infantry under Captains Archie Elder and "Renzie" Brown.

Captain Brown, who, I believe, was the father-in-law of Sam Bruner, the "boss-stiller" at the John E. Day Distillery, lived up the river on the ridge above Josh Carter's place. I remember him as a lean, spry, elderly man with rosy cheeks—always smiling. He was fond of relating war stories, and I hung on his every word. On one occasion he described an encounter with some bushwhackers in which he emphasized the fact that he never fired a shot.

"Why was that, Captain Renzie?" I inquired.

"Because," said he, with a chuckle, "their first bullet knocked off the hammer of my pistol."

One night, sitting near the pot-bellied stove in Glass's Grocery, he revived the long-forgotten tale of the Bridge Hill "Hant." He said that much of the fighting that hot July day in 1862 had occurred around the bridge and that at least one trooper had been buried near its south end. The bridge was a long, covered wooden one—the finest in Kentucky—that spanned Salt River just below the schoolhouse.

It was not long before a story began to be circulated in the community that the dead soldier's spirit had taken up its abode under the bridge's heavy rafters in the dark recesses above and behind the huge, highly arched oaken trusses. He had never been known to hurt anybody but all who had suffered the experience agreed that he was indeed terrifying, even in mere mischief. The "hant" would perch silently on the boot of a buggy, thrust a fleshless arm through the back curtain, slap the unsuspecting driver on the shoulder, and chortle shrilly. Farmers whose land ran down to the river found their cows at early morning already milked dry and so tired they hardly could walk. Some people, highly susceptible to suggestion, claimed they actually had seen the "hant" riding the cows wildly at night when the mist was thick in the bottoms—slapping them with his forage cap on one side and flailing them with the flat of his sword on the other!

One of the most absorbed and, as it turned out, perturbed listeners that evening was a chubby, late-teen-age farm boy we called Skip, who lived across the hills within walking distance of the village. Folks said he was not "real bright" because a horse had kicked him in the head when he was little. Skip had quietly retorted that he knew a lot of people this same horse had kicked. Anyhow, several weeks later on another Saturday night Skip came into Glass's store. He was even then visibly shaken and somewhat incoherent, and he sat closely between two neighbor boys he had persuaded to come with him.

The nerve-shattering adventure he finally related—and which I'm sure he positively believed to his dying day—occurred about as follows: When Mr. Glass had closed his store on the night of Captain Renzie's old ghost tale, Skip had started home. As he trudged along past the icehouses near the schoolyard, he noticed the pale moon hanging less than an hour high on the rim of the valley. Fog poured out of both ends of the bridge as he started through it. He took a few steps, broke into a trot, and tried to whistle. A backward glance—and his heart leaped violently. The specter was floating down from one of the high trusses. It "took in" after him.

Popping out of the bridge Skip hit the steep hill with rapid, desperate strides. Heavy breathing sounded closer. The "hant" was gaining, despite a long sabre, buckled above the pelvis, that banged with hollow rhythm against bare leg bones. With a tremendous spurt Skip dashed around a sharp curve in the hill and raced furiously the few remaining yards to its crest. Looking over his shoulder he saw, to his intense relief, that the road was clear. The spook had quit the contest. It was true then—as Captain Brown had said—that the "hant" never chased anybody beyond sight of the bridge.

With cold sweat oozing from every pore Skip staggered over to the worm fence, lifted himself to the top rail, and drew in the delicious night air with deep gasps. Then his pudgy body stiffened in stark terror. From out of nowhere the "hant" hopped up on the fence beside him and pushed his cap back from a hairless skull. "Whew," the "hant" grinned amiably, "that was some race we had, wasn't it?" In an instant Skip's feet struck the rough macadam, every muscle galvanized for blazing speed never before and not since equaled in Anderson County. "By damn," he shouted back as he spurted up the road, "that ain't nothin' to what we gonna have!"

CHAPTER THREE

The Balky

DURING THE 1890's and the first decade of the present century the Salt River Valley with its adjacent hills was paradise for growing boys: fishing and swimming in summer, hunting, skating, and trapping in winter—woods and fields full of small game and abounding with hickory nuts, walnuts,

Billy Goat

two kinds of grapes, luscious papaws, red and black haws, persimmons, wild plums, and tart crabapples—searching creek beds and adjacent hills for arrow heads and other Indian artifacts in the spring.

One spring we were behind nearly all our neighbors in whitewashing our fence, and my father, usually quite lenient in how and when I performed my chores, was urging me to finish this job. So it was that one Saturday afternoon, my spirits low because the other boys were going on a hunt for arrow heads, I was working on the outside of the picket fence in front of our house. Presently a dirty, mangy dog with white foam dripping from its jaws came trotting down the street toward the river. A few minutes later, a son of the storekeeper came running up and breathlessly announced that the dog which had just passed close to me was "mad" and that it had fallen in a fit and died.

Seizing what seemed to me a sure opportunity to join the arrow head excursion, I rushed into my father's office. "Daddy," I panted, "have you heard about the mad dog? He might have bit me. I bet there are mad dogs all over town. Don't you think it is dangerous for me to be out there whitewashing today?"

"Yes, my son," my father replied with a twinkle in his eye, "it is dangerous for you to be out there on the outside of the fence, right on the street. So close the gate tightly and start on the inside."

My strategy had backfired badly. Not only were my hopes completely blasted, but now I had the inside job with its extra work on runners and posts—a task I had planned to put off on Ole Bill.

I do not remember that we did a great deal of fishing, though there were several good places to fish along the river, like the Cat Hole, the Carter Hole, the Millie Hole—named for one of Holmes Busey's former slaves who had a cabin near there—the Sand Bar, and the Mill Pond at Anderson City. Yet, with but few real fishermen in the village, nobody ever went hungry for fish.

At the end of the millrace was a large fish trap which had been built long before my time by several citizens who lived nearby. During the many years of my professional practice—where I have necessarily encountered much that is petty and mean and selfish in human nature—I have often pondered and marveled over the generous, neighborly unity of this little village where all persons were free, indeed welcome, to visit the fish trap whenever they wished and to take home whatever they found there! At times when the river was high, perch, buffalo suckers, and catfish came down in bushels, almost choking the trap, and the whole community went on what might be called a "fish binge."

I cannot remember when I fired a gun the first time. Evidently I was too small for a regular rifle, so my father found a short, light "ladies'" model .22, and I would ride with him and shoot young rabbits, sitting out in the country roads near twilight on summer afternoons. Later on I hunted squirrels with a Winchester repeating rifle and rabbits and quail with a double-barreled shotgun.

Looking back on it, I do not know why the village boys never hunted on the hill or long ridge just north of the Christian Church. In fact, I was never even back there in all my life. Most of the hunting was along the hills and in the old fields on the south side of the village—the Albert Sherwood, John Moffett, "Uncle" Dick Threlkeld, and "Uncle" Billy Cole farms. My dear friend Ira Moffett, now long deceased, was one of my constant companions in the briar patches and sagebrush where the cottontails were abundant.

However, trapping was the winter sport I loved the best. Each evening was like Christmas eve—you wondered what you'd find in the traps at daybreak next morning! Roy Catlett, one of the sons of the blacksmith—later a fine first baseman on the Glensboro baseball team—was my first trapping partner. I remember with special delight the dozen steel traps we set along the millrace one season where we caught a great many muskrats.

A few winters later Clyde Calvert, son of one of the village storekeepers and later the number one catcher on our team, and I had a string of traps all the way from near the Cat Hole to where Henry Bruner then lived, some distance below the "dripping spring." We also snared rabbits on the hills back of Mr. Sherwood's house near the bridge. One afternoon Calvert set a trap in a huge pile of driftwood and debris near the mill's water wheel—only a stone's throw from his father's store—and, visiting the trap at frequent intervals from dark to bedtime, he caught seven muskrats before the mill began operations next morning!

Just here I must pay my tribute to a big, warmhearted man, without whose kindly interest and gentle tolerance of us small fry, boyhood at Glensboro would not have been what it was. He was the village blacksmith. To us he was "Mr. Catlett"; to grown-ups he was "Bose" Catlett. I do not know what his real first name was—certainly I never heard him called by it.

There was not a youngster in the whole community who did not feel free to go to his shop to make bows and arrows, saw off ends of two-by-fours for "racking blocks," build "rabbit gums," sleds, walking stilts, and other things that caught boyish fancy. It now seems incredible to me that any man, no matter how patient and obliging, could have allowed us to use—and no doubt grossly misuse—his finest cutting tools such as drawing knives, planes, saws, chisels, augers, and hatchets. Yet, Mr. Catlett not only did this, but he looked on with approval and, by his advice and sometimes manual assistance, aided our clumsy, youthful undertakings.

I can see him now, cowhide apron strapped about his waist, sleeves rolled above elbows revealing his sinewy, muscular arms, standing by the glowing forge pumping the huge, dusty, leather bellows and then withdrawing the red-hot metal and beating it into shape with his heavy hammer. Of all the sounds associated with my boyhood, none comes ringing down through the years quite so clearly as the bell-like tones of Bose Catlett's anvil.

When I was about ten years old my father bought me a billy goat. Mr. Catlett reinforced my toy wagon and made a pair of shafts and a singletree. A set of harness came from old buggy lines and bridle reins. It was not very long before the goat was sufficiently trained to pull the wagon around our back yard and in the pasture behind our barn. Then I tried him on the pike in front of our house, and this was all right, too, until we reached the little hill which started in front of the carding factory.

Here my goat positively balked. He would have nothing whatever to do with the hill. When I whipped him, as I finally did, he would bow his neck, thrust his stubby tail straight in the air, rear, and fall backward between the shafts, with his horns almost in my lap!

One afternoon I was trying this stubborn little critter again at the foot of the hill, when "Uncle" John Tindal came along. Uncle John had been a "Salt River Tiger" and was fighting side by side with Henry Clay, Jr., when Clay was killed in the Tigers' celebrated charge at Buena Vista. Now in his vigorous middle eighties—walking three or four miles at least every Saturday from his home across the hills to the village and back—he looked like Santa Claus with his long snow-white whiskers and heavy shock of hair falling down over his coat collar.

Uncle John was vastly amused at the situation. He chuckled a few moments and then asked, "Bill, would you like to know what will make that goat go?"

"I sure would, Uncle John," I replied, "I've tried everything I can think of."

"Well," said Uncle John, "the next time he bows his

neck and just before he starts to stand on his hind legs, you punch him as hard as you can right under the tail with the rough, knotty end of your whip handle. Let's see what happens."

And see we did! I struck the goat rather lightly with my whip and slapped him with the lines. As usual, he bowed his neck, stuck up his tail—and then I let him have it just as Uncle John had said. The effect on that goat was simply astounding! He shivered as if he had been shocked by lightning and leaped forward, bleating hoarsely. I did not even have time to thank Uncle John, because we went up that hill, wagon wheels spinning, as quickly as a squirrel can climb a tree!

A short time after this my poor goat attempted to swallow a green apple whole and choked to death. But, while he lived I never had any more hill trouble. Not that he ever fell in love with that rocky incline—every time we started up, he would slow down and look back. But he had a fine memory. All I had to do was to show him the whip handle and wave it slightly, and then he'd bend to the task without further urging!

CHAPTER FOUR

The Great

THE SALT RIVER Valley of my day was—and I believe still is—an extremely law abiding community. There was complete absence of crime, even of the petty sort. The blacksmith shop stood right beside the pike, but I do not ever recall seeing its doors locked. Many times they were not even closed,

Glensboro Bank Robbery

and I never heard of so much as the loss of a horseshoe nail.

The Valley and adjacent regions were therefore greatly shocked and aroused in the spring of 1906 over a series of depredations which were later found to have been perpetrated by outsiders—men from another county. The banks at Mt. Eden and Van Buren were broken into and combinations on vault doors were battered or blown off, petty cash drawers were rifled, and typewriters and adding machines were carried away. Also several fine horses were stolen in the Valley.

One evening I went with my father to see a sick person who lived in a big white frame house on the road to Van Buren across from what was then—or had been—Vandyck's Mill. We remained there several hours so that the doctor might observe the effect of a certain medicine he had given the patient.

About ten o'clock the grown son came out on the back porch with his shotgun saying that he was going up to the barn, as he had been doing for a week, to guard their gaited saddle stallion, winner of a blue ribbon at the last Lawrenceburg Fair. He had not been gone very long, however, before we heard a muffled report from the direction of the barn and presently the young man returned to the house, completely crestfallen.

He said that he had just climbed up in the hayloft and sat down when he heard talking close to the barn, then someone unlatching the front door of the shed and stealthily entering the front stall. Cocking his gun, he started to climb down the ladder, when—to his utter dismay—the weapon accidentally went off with a loud bang. For a few moments he clung to the ladder in shock, then he jumped down and ran to the door. In the dim starlight he saw two men making top speed across the barn lot toward the road.

Glensboro, Kentucky, in 1904. Salt River lies in the foreground.

The Townsend family about 1900

The lot was separated from the pike by a very old rock fence. Through the years it had settled, and soil had washed down from the adjoining hillside until the fence was only about two feet above the ground. In order to keep his stock from jumping out of the lot, the farmer had run two strands of barbed wire supported by thin scantlings set far apart along the top of the rock wall. Apparently the horse thieves did not see the wire, because they ran headlong into it as they attempted to leap over the rock fence. Then, after some scuffling and much cussing, they detached themselves and "lit out" up the pike.

The farmer's son thought the men might have left some identifying clues, so we took a lantern and went back to the barn lot. Here we found ample evidence of the thieves' entanglement in the fence. Long strips of cloth hung on the wires. Several barbs were bloody, and impaled on one of them was a messy piece of scalp about the size of a silver dollar with heavy strands of brick-red hair dangling from it. Beside the fence was a new felt hat with the label of a Shelbyville store on the inside. Ultimately these clues greatly assisted in the capture of the culprits, but not before the occurrence of what was to become known as the "Great Glensboro Bank Robbery."

One Saturday afternoon Mr. W. L. Franklin, cashier of the new Farmers Bank, took me bird hunting with his two brown-and-white setters. Being an excellent shot, he got his bag without difficulty, while I "fired and fell back" with more energy than accuracy and, of course, without much decrease in the quail population.

That night about eleven o'clock I was awakened when I heard my father speaking in guarded tones over the lowered upper sash of his bedroom window that opened out onto the front porch. Thinking he was talking to somebody about a patient, as he frequently did, I was drifting off to sleep again when he asked my mother where my shotgun was. After he had dressed and the front door slammed, I put on my clothes as quickly as I could, took my father's .38 Smith and Wesson from a dresser drawer, and stepped outside.

There in the middle of the road stood Mr. Franklin, who had been on our porch, with his pump gun, and Delbert Catlett, son of the blacksmith, who had a revolver. Catlett was repeating to my father, who was president of the bank, what he had previously told Franklin. He said that he had been out late and was putting up his horse in a barn on the street just west of the bank when he heard a dull noise. Looking out in the moonlight toward the bank, he saw that its back door was standing wide open. Thinking instantly of what recently had happened at Mt. Eden and Van Buren, he had hurried around to Mr. Franklin's house, which stood next to the bank, and informed him of the suspicious situation. Franklin was absolutely positive that he had locked this door the last thing he did before leaving the bank.

My father seemed considerably annoyed at my sudden, unexpected, and uninvited appearance, but he finally acknowledged my presence sufficiently to direct me to go down the street and wake up Mr. Calvert, the storekeeper, and "Uncle" George Hawkins, the miller. This I did, and, adequately armed, they soon joined the group on the pike.

The "posse" now having been organized, my father directed Catlett and me to go around through Franklin's side yard and to get behind a high pile of cordwood stacked near the bank's back-yard fence. Franklin and his pump gun would go along with us. When we had done this, we could hear the rest of the party fling open the front door of the building and rush inside.

At this point everything was in semidarkness again. Then Catlett nudged me and whispered, "Don't you see somebody crawling near the door?" "Yeah, somebody's on the floor," I replied through chattering teeth.

Suddenly Mr. Franklin shouted loudly, "Hold on! Hold on! Don't shoot! My bird dogs are in there!"

In another instant the two brown-and-white setters scampered down the steps and ran back into the coal house where Mr. Franklin had put them before dark the previous afternoon. Examination showed that the cashier had indeed turned the key in the lock; but the bolt had not caught in the metal groove, and the strong west wind had blown the back door open.

Well, I count it a red letter day when I have an opportunity to go back home for a brief visit with old friends and schoolmates—now unfortunately all too few. And I never pass the little brick building that once was the Farmers Bank without thinking of the Great Glensboro Bank Robbery.

CHAPTER FIVE

The Country

THE COUNTRY DOCTOR—now practically extinct—was indeed a rugged individualist. He had to be—with no hospitals, no laboratory technicians, no antibiotics, no trained nurses, no anesthetists. He was strictly on his own.

My father, for many years the only doctor at

Doctor

Glensboro, served—with a buggy and three horses—an area of approximately twenty square miles. There were no other doctors closer than Dr. Gibbs at Fox Creek, Dr. Simpson at Sinai, Dr. Adams at Johnsonville, Dr. Gilbert at Van Buren, and Dr. Shouse at Mt. Eden.

Country doctors' fees were extremely moderate, according to present-day standards—$1.00 for office calls; $2.00, regardless of distance, for day house calls; $3.00, no distance limit, for night house calls; $8.00 for child delivery. No bills were ever sent out, and no patient ever asked to pay one. Moreover, the doctor would get up in the middle of the night and drive five or six miles in a blinding snowstorm to see a patient he knew would never be able to pay him a penny!

And fees did not have to be paid in cash. Some of the doctors had farms—my father had a couple up the valley at Anderson City—and if cash was scarce or non-existent, as it frequently was, payment in hay, grain, and livestock was quite acceptable. Sometimes the patient and his family had neither money nor anything else to use in lieu of it; but they never forgot the debt. Long after my father's death people would come into my law office and say apologetically that they had owed the doctor for many years a bill which until then they had been unable to pay. Did I have his ledger which would show the exact amount? When that had been ascertained, these honest Andersonians would hand out the cash, take their receipt, and start happily homeward, conscious that a long-standing obligation was at last fully discharged.

One task the country doctor especially hated was pulling teeth. He realized he was no dental surgeon, but sometimes the job had to be done without delay. Even when I was a small boy most roads were turn-pikes improved with rough macadam, but some were in their original state of clay and dirt—and very muddy in winter. On these roads my father had to ride horseback when the weather was bad, and I rode with him, when I was not more than seven or eight years old, on a small, gentle horse, called "Old Pony." On these trips I first saw him pull teeth—frequently without dismounting from his horse!

He would be riding, for instance, down what was then called the "Old State Road," starting from where Billy Best lived on the Pleasant Grove ridge and running over to the Crooked Creek pike. A farmer would come out of his house, halt my father, and say: "Doc, I've got an old tooth that's nearly killing me—never slept a wink all night." My father would examine his mouth as he came up close to the withers of the big black "run an' walker"—then fumble in his saddle-pockets, take out a vicious looking pair of forceps, sterilize them with a little bottle of alcohol, lean over and put his left arm around the patient's neck, and, assisted by the leverage, yank the tooth quickly, if not painlessly.

"Now," said my father, "if that place gets to jumping, just lay your quid of tobacco on it."

"O.K., Doc," the relieved farmer would reply, and we'd ride on.

The country doctor worked night and day, with no vacations. No wonder he frequently died while still in his prime. I've known my father to go for three days and nights without sleeping in a bed. I remember once he delivered four babies between dark and sunup, and the mothers lived miles from each other.

I shall always cherish with warm remembrance the wonderfully cooperative spirit and strong friendship that existed among these dedicated men. One summer Dr. Shouse of Mt. Eden came down with a desperate illness. My father went out there and remained constantly at his bedside for a week. And during his own last illness, Drs. Shouse, C. N. Kavanaugh, and Gibbs did the same for him.

Frequently the doctors conferred with each other in serious cases. This was especially true of my father and Dr. Shouse and Dr. Kavanaugh of Lawrenceburg. Kavanaugh had a son, Charles, Jr., called Mike, who was a few years older than I. He and I were going to be doctors and therefore we went along on many of these consultation trips. Mike later had a brilliant career as a physician with the Lexington Clinic; but the Townsend boy was sidetracked at the Lexington courthouse!

These doctors did not attempt surgery beyond the bare necessity of the occasion—such as amputation of a finger, hand, arm, or occasionally a leg. Patients needing abdominal or other than simple surgery were taken to Lexington or Louisville, sometimes with more hardship on the family physician than on the patient. I recall one occasion when my father was taking an appendix case to Louisville in a new Stanley Steamer ambulance operated by a driver not very well skilled in this new-fangled method of transportation. Just this side of Shelbyville the conveyance ran off the road and rolled down a ten-foot bank, the patient, who weighed two hundred and fifty pounds, falling on top of the doctor. Upon reaching Louisville it was necessary to hospitalize two patients instead of one!

When surgery was required, lack of facilities and assistance did not deter any of these doctors from the immediate performance of his duty. The dining room table was moved into the kitchen and extra leaves put in it. A clean white sheet was spread over the top. Instruments were sterilized in a dishpan on the wood burning stove and the teakettle was brought to a boil. A cone was made from an old magazine or newspaper and a napkin or handkerchief saturated with chloroform was dropped in it. The housewife stood by with a kerosene lamp turned as high as the frequently untrimmed wick would permit. When the patient was "under," the doctor calmly went to work with knife and saw; and, when the anesthetic got "thin"—as indicated by groan or flinch—the doctor would drop his instruments, give the prostrate form a few more whiffs from the cone, and then resume the operation.

Before I was past my middle teens I became acutely aware of the fact that these men who literally were giving their lives to their profession were something less than enthusiastic about any reflections upon it—no matter how facetiously made. This, however, was true of city doctors as well as their brethren from the country.

Drs. A. M. Cartledge and Louis Frank, Sr., of Louisville were, during the first decade of the century, two of the most noted surgeons in the Ohio River Valley. Both were classmates of my father in medical college, and Cartledge had been his roommate. One time they invited him to the annual Louisville Medical Society banquet and generously consented to let me come with him. Seeking to avoid the usual stereotyped program the committee on arrangements had procured a layman noted as a humorist to deliver the principal address. His opening remark was: "We have the allopath, the homeopath, and the osteopath—but all the paths lead but to the grave!" From audience reactions I gained the distinct impression that this witticism was not generally regarded as sufficiently funny to have justified the selection of this particular guest speaker!

No one in his right mind will even attempt to deny the marvelous boon conferred upon mankind by the specialist of today. Lives are constantly saved and people restored to health because of skill and knowledge acquired through the intensive study of a particular segment of the human body. And yet, these specialists are the first to admit that the old country doctor, practicing for years among a population that hardly ever shifted, possessed certain advantages nobody else can ever acquire. He knew his patient—he saw him all in one piece—as a whole. More likely than not he had been present at his birth—frequently at the births of his father and mother, his brothers and sisters and cousins. He knew his background and heredity. Once I remember my father saying to my mother about a young girl—nervous, undernourished, not doing well in school—whom he had just examined: "She is just like her mother was at her age. She'll be all right with proper attention"—and this prediction proved correct.

Also, the country doctor was a sort of father confessor to the whole community on domestic, economic, and other matters wholly unassociated with the practice of medicine. His advice and assistance—all given gratis—were sought on almost every conceivable subject. And sometimes requests came most unexpectedly and in the midst of sorrow and tragedy. One summer several members of a prominent family that lived over on the Lawrenceburg-Bardstown road fell ill with typhoid fever. One daughter, Sally, a beautiful girl in her late teens, was gravely ill. My father had been there for a night and two days; but, near sundown on the second day, it was unmistakably apparent that, though fully conscious, she was sinking rapidly. No minister being available, the distraught parents asked the doctor to say a few words of comfort; and the doctor—not a member of any church—knelt by the bedside, bowed his head upon the quilted coverlet, and prayed fervently.

CHAPTER SIX

House Parties

HOUSE PARTIES were all the rage by the time I went to college. The motor era was in its early stages and cars were not familiar to the public generally. Therefore, since frequent contacts among young folks living at a distance from each other were not easy or convenient, the house party served a *and Black-Eyed Susans*

unique social need. Usually it was not merely a weekend affair. More likely it lasted for a week or, at least, four or five days.

Of all of these, the Routt house parties were distinctly in a class by themselves. The Claiborne Routt farm, of some seven or eight hundred acres, lay just north of the Lawrenceburg-Bardstown road in the direction of Glensboro. The big house was a picturesque, rambling, story-and-a-half structure made of huge walnut and poplar hand-hewn logs, neatly weatherboarded and painted white with green shutters. It had wide, wood-burning fireplaces, spacious hearths, and tall outside chimneys of dressed limestone. Three or four generations of the family had been born there, and the house was filled with beautiful antiques and heirlooms that had stood in one place for more than a century.

At that time the young people of the family consisted of Elizabeth and her sister Rose—several years younger than Elizabeth—three brothers, all in college with me—Grover, Seneca, and Bill, the latter well-known for many years as the Anderson County Clerk. About twice each summer, or sometimes oftener, the Routts would "blow a blast on the ram's horn" which all invited friends heard with clarity and accepted with alacrity!

One frequent guest, Bob McBrayer, the only son of Lucien McBrayer, the Lawrenceburg banker, shared in an incident that taught me a lesson—though it came near being a severe one—in the handling of automatic firearms. Bob's father had just bought him a new .32 calibre Colt's automatic pistol. We had been out in the Routt's back yard shooting at a target. Returning to the house, we sat on the front porch, and I asked Bob to let me see the gun. As he handed it to me, I inquired if it was loaded, to which he replied in the negative, showing me how he had removed from the handle the clip which contained the cartridges. We had forgotten, however, that the firing of our final shot had also thrust the last cartridge into the barrel and that, therefore, the gun was not only loaded but cocked!

My father had long ago impressed me with the fact that I must not—under any circumstances whatever—point a weapon in the direction of any person, and at this time such firm instructions may have prevented a real tragedy. However, I did point the pistol and sight it at trees and other inanimate objects and, finally, at my horse, not yet unharnessed and still hitched to the fence. Then suddenly, to the utter consternation of all of us, the thing went off and buried a copper-jacket bullet in a post only a few inches from my horse's head! I had few secrets from my father—not even the college escapades that, among other things equally justifiable, kept me from ever being a favorite of that stern old disciplinarian, President James K. Patterson; but I have no recollection of telling him about the stupid incident which nearly caused the death of one of his favorite "nags."

Healthy appetites were abundantly satisfied by delectable food at the Routt house parties. Those breakfasts: old hickory-smoked ham and bacon, eggs fresh from the henhouse, hot, fluffy biscuits, yesterday's golden butter churned in the kitchen, tart damson preserves and jelly from the large plum tree near the front porch, sorghum molasses on mush fried in "red-eye" gravy, coffee with aroma just released from the grinder, and cream so rich and thick that it could be skimmed from a crock with a fork!

Fun and more fun was the order of the days and nights. Mrs. Routt had passed away at this time, but the father, bless him, was not only in favor of all the "goings-on," but was ever ready to lend a hand in genial promotion. There were horseback rides, Mr. Routt actually taking horses from work on the farm; picnics at the mineral spring near Goodnight's bridge on Salt River; hay rides on moonlit evenings and leisurely strolls along the narrow, winding turnpike to the country store. All the Routts were musical, Elizabeth later having a successful singing career in Louisville and New York. Both girls played the piano. At college the three Routt boys and I, calling ourselves the Pewter Spoon Quartet, had achieved some small notice—favorable or otherwise—in vocal harmonizing of the "barber shop" variety. So in the evenings when nothing else was on the entire house party, with Rose at the keyboard, would gather around the piano and "give out" with current favorites such as "The Druid's Altar," all about a sylvan paradise where the Druids—those sprightly, elfin magicians of the old Welsh and Irish sagas—performed their rituals.

It so happened that, right on the Routt farm, down through a meadow gorgeous with black-eyed Susans, near the foot of a gentle, wooded slope, there was a prodigal display of scenic nature which would have made any Druid forget the hallowed groves of Wales or the sainted dells of Killarney! Luxuriant vegetation

Glensboro School, 1896. Professor Ezra L Gillis is standing at the right; the author is third from the left in the bottom row.

The author as a State College senior

was rooted in a deep black loam. Forest trees of red oak, yellow poplar, sugar maple, walnut, blue ash, and the smooth, brittle-barked beech on which initials could be so easily carved harbored cardinals, wood thrushes, bluebirds, and mocking birds, and footpaths were carpeted with the fallen, richly tinted leaves of many autumns. A tiny brook meandered down the rocky bed of a narrow, shallow ravine lined with honeysuckle, trumpet vines, and forget-me-nots, and across the brook a large, silvery beech had fallen; here we could sit, pull off our shoes, and wriggle bare toes in the cool, placid stream.

One recent autumn, on my way to Hodgenville, I turned aside at the country store, still standing in the forks of the road, and drove slowly down the familiar little pike to what was formerly the Routt farm. It was a mistake I shall not make again.

The fine old house was gone—burned—without even a pile of ashes to show where it stood. The forest trees and the prone silvery beech were long ago victims of the sawmill's insatiable maw. Cornstalks—without so much as a flapping scarecrow to vary the monotony of the dreary landscape—rustled moodily where the wild flowers had grown. Relentless plowing had destroyed the brook, and crystal waters trickled over moss-grown stones no more.

But the Routt house parties will never be forgotten. And the happy, carefree guests who so hugely enjoyed them will live on in memory—forever young, untouched by time—as long as life shall last.

CHAPTER SEVEN

The Salt

THE SALT RIVER Valley was an absorbing place for anybody interested in American history. When I was growing up six or seven veterans of the Mexican War still were living and amazingly spry. All of them were called "Uncle." I remember John Tindal, Dick Threlkeld, Curt Crutcher,

River Tigers

who in earlier days was the village cobbler, Dick Shouse, Taylor Husband, and my great-uncle, Sanford Brown.

Uncle Curt had brought his musket home from the army, and I loved to go to his little cottage—on the opposite side of the street from where my cherished friends, Athel and Ollie Gash, now live—and to visit with him and his sweet old wife, "Aunt Rhody," holding fondly the rusty, long-barreled, muzzle-loading weapon across my knees all the while.

Frequently on Saturday afternoons several of the "Salt River Tigers" would play checkers under a large locust tree that stood close to the end of the porch of Butler Sullivan's store, across from the Christian Church. On such occasions I would sit for hours on the nearby rock wall—which is still intact and sturdy—entranced with their reminiscences of the supreme adventure of their lives.

When war broke out with Mexico an infantry outfit was recruited in Anderson County—largely from the Valley and adjacent regions—which was officially designated as Company "C," Second Regiment, Kentucky Volunteers, but which went down in battle annals as "The Salt River Tigers." The colonel of the Second Kentucky was William R. McKee of Midway, and its Lieutenant Colonel was Henry Clay, Jr., son of the Sage of Ashland, who had graduated from West Point, but later resigned to practice law in Louisville. The regiment was mustered in on June 9, 1846, at Louisville and was sent at once to Mexico.

Its finest hour came at the battle of Buena Vista. The Mexican Army under General Santa Anna arrived on the field about noon on February 22, 1847. His troops outnumbered General Taylor's Americans by more than four to one, and Santa Anna lost no time in demanding Taylor's surrender, which was promptly declined. A few hours later the engagement began, and the battle raged until dark.

Next morning it was renewed with greater intensity, and things were going badly for the Americans when Colonel McKee rode up to Lieutenant Colonel Clay and informed him that General Taylor had just ordered the Second Kentucky to assault Santa Anna's right flank. McKee directed Clay to select the company to spearhead the attack. Without hesitation Clay picked the "Salt River Tigers," who immediately sprang forward in a wild, plunging bayonet charge that broke the enemy's lines and was largely responsible for causing the Mexicans to retreat during the night, leaving over five hundred of their dead on the field. But the victory had been a costly one. Many of the "Tigers" and other soldiers of the Second Kentucky, including both McKee and Clay, were killed, and many more were wounded.

Of course, during my boyhood Civil War veterans were plentiful, lots of them not having reached three-score and ten. There were a few Union soldiers, but most of these veterans were Confederates, and practically all of them were John Morgan's men of the Fifth Kentucky Cavalry, of whom the Federal General W. T. Sherman wrote General Halleck: "War suits them, and the rascals are brave; fine riders, bold to rashness, and are the most dangerous set of men which this War has turned loose upon the world." I never tired of hearing John Moffett, Albert Sherwood, and others talk about Shiloh, Hartsville, Murfreesboro, the two great raids into Kentucky, and the disastrous invasion of Ohio.

One incident, involving an exchange of communications with the enemy and which amused even General Morgan, occurred when they attempted to cross Green River at the Tebb's Bend bridge on July 4, 1863. It was defended by the Twenty-fifth Michigan Infantry under Colonel Orlando H. Moore. After firing a heavy artillery salvo at the Union troops, Morgan sent Lieutenant Joe Tucker of Harrisonville forward under truce flag with the following message: "Dear Colonel: I demand your immediate, unconditional surrender." The colonel sat down on a log and wrote back: "Dear General: I'd rather not." Thereafter Morgan made three desperate attacks against the entrenched Michigan infantrymen, but all resulted in bloody repulse.

It was from Sherwood that I first heard about the effort to involve the first lieutenant of their company in the robbery of the Farmers' Bank at Mt. Sterling. On June 8, 1864, General Morgan, during his last foray into the Bluegrass, captured Mt. Sterling after routing the Union forces in a brisk engagement. Before the Confederates left that town on their way to Lexington the bank was robbed of a large sum of money. Several months thereafter Lieutenant James F. Witherspoon, who owned a fine farm in Anderson County, apparently the only one of Morgan's men who had property that could be quickly seized, was sued by the bank in the Anderson Circuit Court. Still in the army and absent from the state, Witherspoon did not know of this action, nor of the charges brought against him, until the bank had obtained judgment and his farm had been sold!

Luckily, before the court had confirmed the sale Witherspoon heard of the proceedings, employed a lawyer, filed his answer, and proved by Sherwood and Pleas Oliver, both from Camden–now Glensboro–and other witnesses that he had been in no way connected with the robbery. The Circuit Court, however, declined to set the sale aside, and Witherspoon's counsel then appealed successfully to the Court of Appeals.

One of the first decisions of the Court of Appeals I looked up when I entered the Law College of the University of Kentucky was Witherspoon *vs.* Farmers' Bank of Mt. Sterling, 63 Kentucky Reports, 496. The judgment against him had, indeed, been a large one–$59,057.33. But that sturdy old Unionist, Chief Justice George Robertson, speaking for the court, said that there was "no evidence tending to prove that Witherspoon, in any way, counseled, aided or even approved the robbery of the bank." On the contrary, proof by several witnesses showed he had nothing to do with it, "either before or after its perpetration."

The Chief Justice said, further, that the ruling of the lower court evidently had been based on the mere fact that the lieutenant had "aided in the capture of Mt. Sterling," but he said that "capture of the town itself was not, in the military sense, an unlawful act. It was not forbidden, but allowed by the laws of war between antagonist parties recognized as belligerents." The court, however, did castigate severely the unidentified members of Morgan's command who had committed the "reprehensible act" against the bank.

Well, all this had its aftermath. I had not been long at the Fayette County Bar before I met Miss Nellie Morgan, an elderly spinster—the general's only surviving niece. Miss Nellie was a kind, gentle old lady—except when engaged in defending the name and fame of "Uncle John." To her, "Uncle John" was a chivalrous knight in shining armor, personally immaculate in thought and deed, who tolerated from his men not the slightest deviation from the strictest rules of honor!

One day in the early thirties she came into my office and, after a few words of general conversation, she suddenly became very serious and said: "Mr. Townsend, I have been reading your book on the Civil War in Kentucky, and you say that some of Uncle John's men robbed the bank at Mt. Sterling. What is your authority for that statement?"

"Miss Nellie," I replied, "I got my information from the Kentucky Reports."

She sniffed contemptuously, looked out the window a moment, took a pad and pencil from her hand bag, and then inquired, "What did you say is the name of that little pamphlet?"

I explained that the Kentucky Reports were no pamphlets, but bulky volumes bound in sheepskin, in which were published the official decisions of the highest court in our state. I took down volume sixty-three of the Reports and showed her where the court had decided, as facts admitted in the record, that, on June 8, 1864, General Morgan had captured Mt. Sterling and that "immediately after the capitulation, one of his subaltern officers and a small band of his soldiers forcibly entered the vault of the bank" and took away approximately $60,000.00.

Still unconvinced and much outraged, Miss Nellie left my office and, as I later learned, went straight to another law office and requested to see volume sixty-three of the Reports, so that she might be sure I had not rung in some "phony" pages on her!

But this was not all. Several weeks later she came back, and this time she brought along Captain J. Esten Keller, a grand old man who had served on Morgan's staff. "Mr. Townsend," she said without any preliminaries, "I hear that you have quoted the newspapers as saying that some of Uncle John's men robbed the bank at Georgetown. Now, I met Captain Keller on the street just now and he tells me positively that Uncle John's soldiers never took a penny from the bank at Georgetown, and he was right there—isn't that so, Captain Keller?"

The captain's eyes twinkled, and I knew he had something up his sleeve. "Why, yes indeed, Miss Nellie," he replied, "but I don't believe I told you why we never took any money from the bank. The truth of the business is that after we broke in the building and blew the safe, we found that when we ran the damyankees out of town the scoundrels had taken away all the cash and hauled it to Frankfort, and we couldn't find a single cent!"

CHAPTER EIGHT

The Sun Stroke

WHEN I WAS a youngster tobacco was raised—as now—on most farms in our region. Yet its use, one way or another, by teenagers was nothing at all like it is today. At least, such is true around Lexington and, I believe, in the Bluegrass gen-

Chew of Tobacco

erally. I can remember only one boy of my age, or maybe a little older, at our school in Glensboro who chewed tobacco. He was an extremely likeable chap, Fred Cole, son of "Uncle" Billy Cole, on whose farm we hunted frequently and were always welcome. To most of the school kids, my nickname was "Hickory Bill," or just plain "Hickory"; but Uncle Billy Cole always called me "Doctor Bill."

I shall never cease to remember my first and last chew of tobacco. One blazingly hot, sultry July day when I was about fourteen my father sent me with a wheelbarrow down the alley on which our barn was located to get a sack of "ship-stuff" from the mill to feed our meat hogs. On my way I came upon my old friend Ben Warford, who was digging postholes in a fence line. I stopped, sat down on one of the handles of the wheelbarrow, and chatted with Ben for a few minutes. During our conversation, he pulled a thick plug of Battle Axe tobacco from his overalls pocket and bit off a large chunk which he began chewing with great relish, shifting it from one cheek to the other and back again.

Unable to stand the tempting sight any longer, I said, "Ben, how about giving me a little taste of that Battle Axe?" Obligingly, he handed me the plug, and I put my teeth into it. Finding it very sweet, I probably took a bigger chew than I realized. Anyway, I soon resumed my trip to the mill; but, before I got there, I realized that the stuff had greatly excited the flow of saliva and, although I was spitting frequently, I was also swallowing some of the licorice-laden juice. About this time, I threw the quid away, but the damage already was done. By the time my sack was filled I was feeling woozy, and I barely made it back to the barn, threw the "ship-stuff" in the corn crib, staggered down the gravel walk to the house, and collapsed on the sofa in the hall.

At this point my father came in from his office in the corner of the yard, and my mother said to him, very sharply, "Now, look what you've done. You sent this child down to the mill this hot day and he's had a sun stroke!" My father looked at me, lying there pale and limp. Then he bent over me, felt my pulse, lifted my eyelids and looked at the pupils. I've always been sure he also smelled the tobacco on my breath. But he didn't give me away. "No, he hasn't had a sun stroke," he told my mother, reassuringly. "Something seems to have upset him a little, but he'll soon be all right." And he was correct.

The ready made cigarette was not then on sale at the country stores, although, a little later, a few Sweet Caporals appeared in small quantities. The cigarette smoker had to roll his own with Natural Leaf, put up in a red bag, or Bull Durham, in a white sack.

I do not recall that any of the boys about my age—Ira Moffett, Roy Catlett, Clyde Calvert, Hubert Ragan, Herbert Gordon, Walter Hawkins, or Leo Gibbs—used tobacco in any form. My father believed that inhaling tobacco smoke was especially bad for growing youngsters, and I promised him that I would not smoke cigarettes, and I never have. Of course, we sometimes puffed on pieces of dead grape vines, corn silks, and the cotton-like bloom of a weed called "Life Everlasting," but this was about the extent of our indulgence until we were past sixteen, or maybe much older.

One day my father informed me that next morning we would leave for Louisville to buy me some fall clothes. When I told my friend and trapping partner, Calvert—who is just two weeks my senior—about this, he wanted to go along; his father was willing, and we were glad to have him. Early that evening, I said to Clyde, "Now, this is a special occasion we must celebrate. Before your father closes his store tonight you get a couple of Daniel Boone cigars and, going down on the train, we'll slip away somehow and smoke 'em." Clyde thought this was a capital idea and proceeded accordingly.

Shortly after our train had passed Avenstoke, while my father was absorbed in reading the *Courier-Journal*, Calvert and I began wandering through the several coaches, passing our seats now and then. Finally everything seemed to be in good shape so we stopped in the "smoker," lit up, and pulled lustily and rapidly on the cigars until they were about two-thirds consumed and no longer tasted as good as they did at the start.

Then we threw the stumps out the window and returned to the coach where Dad, apparently, still was interested in his newspaper. In congratulating ourselves that we had escaped discovery we forgot that one did not need to enter the "smoker" in order to see inside. This could very easily be done by standing on the platform and looking through the glass panels of the coach door.

Arriving in Louisville about noon we went immediately to the Old Vienna Restaurant on Fourth Street, north of Main, a delightful place with high mahogany wainscoating and large crystal chandeliers, which specialized in seafood. Dad gave the waiter three large orders for fried oysters, of which he knew I was usually very fond. But today Clyde and I were badly "off feed," and my father expressed such surprise and was so solicitous that we clean up our plates that I began to suspect he knew something he had not told us and, in fact, never did tell us.

My worst suspicions were confirmed when, after paying the bill, he walked over to the tobacco counter and bought three cigars instead of one. With the utmost nonchalance, he put one of the cigars in his mouth and shoved the other two across the glass-topped case to Clyde and me. Then, to be sure they were smoked—for which at that time we certainly had not the slightest desire—he lighted his cigar and kept the same match burning for ours. With our red faces, abashed manner, and awkward handling of this newly acquired symbol of young manhood—none of which my father seemed to notice—we walked slowly, and not very happily, up Market Street to Levy Brothers clothing store. I have always believed my father saw us smoking the cigars, and the fact that I was levelling with him about cigarettes was largely responsible for his equanimity on this occasion.

I did not start regular smoking until I came to college. Here the owner of a calabash pipe had reached the very height of sophistication! Of course cigars came next, and gradually the tobacco habit crept up on me until before I reached my early forties I was smoking about ten cigars a day, with a pipe in between—if any such interval existed. For a long time I tried to cut down. I criticized myself severely. Of evenings I would firmly resolve to smoke only five cigars next day. Then when morning came I would remind myself that I was not committed or limited to any particular part of the day, and therefore I could smoke four during the morning and the fifth after lunch. This I would do, and then for the remainder of the day and during the evening I would be utterly bereft!

I found also that an excessive user of tobacco, in most cases, tends to become a sort of prima donna. He gets very finicky—everything must be just right. Cigars, with wrappers carefully removed, must be laid in a large humidor with a small glass of apple brandy at each end to give them moisture superior to water and a wonderful flavor!

One evening, I sat at home smoking a new pipe. I had completely failed to reduce to any extent whatever my consumption of the "noxious weed." I looked down, and the front of my coat was covered with big splotches of ashes and I had burned a small hole in my vest. Suddenly I threw my pipe on the flaming logs in the fireplace, and my precious cigars followed it.

Well, it was especially tough for the first two months. I had not realized how much the hands had to do with the habit. I could not resist putting my fingers to my lips until I began stretching and wriggling rubber bands when the hand-to-mouth impulse came.

That has been a good many years ago, and while the acute suffering was of comparatively short duration I still envy my friends who can be conservative in their smoking. Nothing can equal the fragrance and satisfaction of a fine after-dinner cigar nor the sweetness of a well broken in pipe filled with Walnut, London Dock, or some other aromatic blend.

It did not occur to me that temperament had played an important part in my "all or nothing" experience with tobacco until—quite a long time after this—I went to the Mayo Clinic at Rochester, Minnesota, for a physical checkup. In the final interview with my main consultant, he said to me, "In the battles of life, you do not choose your techniques wisely. To illustrate, you use the same weapon to kill a gnat that one would use in fighting an elephant. In the latter instance, it would, of course, be necessary to go 'all out'; but, in the former, the job ought to be done with a minimum of effort and with complete relaxation."

I've tried to remember what the doctor said and to follow his advice, but I do not believe I have been very successful.

CHAPTER NINE

The Mysterious

WHEN COLLEGE TIME came nobody was ever as hard to wean away from his native hills and valley as I was. The first time I enrolled in college I had been in school five days when my father made a psychological blunder he never re-

Disappearance of Willis E. Smith

peated. I received a letter from him saying that "the old buggy was empty." There was just time enough to catch the afternoon train to Lawrenceburg. Next morning the old buggy wasn't empty any more!

The second time was worse than the first. Like the

cat dropped in the road that beats its owner home, I almost did just that. My father and I came over to Lexington, went to a show at the Opera House that evening, stayed all night at the Phoenix Hotel, and next morning went out to the college. Having presumably fixed me up out there, he took the morning train back to Lawrenceburg.

Shortly before supper time that evening his phone rang, and when he answered he was no doubt greatly startled to hear his son's voice say, "Hello, Dad." "Where are you?" he asked quickly. "Oh, I'm here in Lawrenceburg," I replied cheerily. For a moment there was shocked silence on the phone. Then he said, "All right, I'll send Charlie Tindall for you as soon as I can find him." Finally, on the third try, I managed to stay, but only by coming home every Friday night and returning Sunday afternoon for the first six months!

Incidentally, it is strange how phobias like this will linger with you. Years later, when my daughter—an only child as I was—started to Vassar I bought her a round trip ticket on the C. & O. Vividly remembering my own nostalgia, I said to her, "Now, if you don't like it up there, you come right back home." During the next three weeks I lost fifteen pounds in my struggle with dreadfully mixed emotions. I knew she ought to stay, but I also realized for the first time just what my father meant when he wrote that "the old buggy was empty"! Fortunately, her self-control was much better than mine had been, and she very happily remained at Poughkeepsie and graduated in the class of 1937.

"State College," as the University was then known, had a very small enrollment when I went there. President Patterson, called "He Pat" behind his back, was an imperious autocrat. His brother Walter, who—it was said—had never been to college, called "She Pat," was Principal of the "Academy." The President's son William, a hard-drinking, indifferent student nicknamed "It Pat," had died years before my time, but his remarkable skill as a crap shooter had become a campus legend.

He Pat never visualized the institution as anything more than a little school, with himself as headmaster. Everything revolved around him. For instance, every entrance card must pass across his desk, and none escaped his keen old eyes. This fact resulted in the first of my all-too-many run-ins with him. In filling out my entrance blank I was seized with a brash impulse which occasionally and unaccountably afflicts teenagers, and I answered the question about my religious affiliation with the word "Buddhist." Next day, having seen my card, He Pat summoned me to his office. I had not the slightest idea that the purpose of this invitation was to extend effusive personal greetings to the Asiatic lad who was the first foreign student ever to register at State College! But when He Pat discovered that I was a young squirt who had never lived more than thirty-five miles from the Administration Building, he lectured me severely on the rules of propriety and the fitness of things!

So with this inauspicious start and other intervening irritations, my rating with Dr. Patterson already was exceedingly low when—quite a bit later—I became involved in an episode which the local newspapers headlined as "The Mysterious Disappearance of Willis E. Smith." L. E. Smith was a serious minded, slightly eccentric upperclassman from Southwest Kentucky. That fall he brought back his younger brother Willis E. and entered him as a freshman. They lived with Mrs. Beauchamp, noted suffragette and temperance leader, at her home just outside the city limits on the Versailles Pike, where they worked part time for board and lodging.

One day, about a week after school began, the older Smith notified college authorities that his brother was missing and gave the Lexington police his photograph and physical description. Shortly thereafter things took a serious turn indeed. An old lady who ran a boarding house near the corner of South Limestone and Euclid Avenue, where the Holmes dormitory for girls is now located, told police that on the night of Smith's disappearance she had been sitting on her front porch watching a group of college boys hazing one or more freshmen. She could see them very plainly because of the bright arc light at the street intersection.

Suddenly a boy broke away, started to run, and another boy she couldn't identify threw a fragment of brick at him. The fleeing youth fell, and the whole group hastily carried off the prostrate form. The victim, she said, looked like the picture of Smith. Did she know anybody in the group? Yes, she recognized Bill Townsend and two other boys who had once boarded with her.

Of course we were not only dumbfounded by this tale, but positively aghast when we heard that He Pat—who was then on a change-of-work status—had been put in charge of the college investigation! And, as we so greatly feared, our interview with him was far worse than our talks with the police. He was really "laying" for us. He referred to us as a trio of miscreants who were turning out just like he always knew we would. He had a formidable list of high crimes and misdemeanors of long standing which he said he had reason to believe—but had not yet been able to prove—we had committed. I can remember only a few. We had made soup out of some of his prize chickens that roosted in the barn back of his house; we had tied the dump-cart mule to the lectern on the chapel rostrum at Halloween; and he felt sure that, a few nights before summer vacation, we had tried to make "Old Rollo," the gray horse he drove to a phaeton on his daily afternoon rides, look like a zebra by shearing his mane and tail and striping his dappled hide with black paint!

And then, the utterly humorless old Scotchman added a piece of information at which—nervous and distraught though we were—we found it difficult to keep straight faces. Deadly serious, with voice quivering, he told us that the colored boys he had hired to scrub Old Rollo with turpentine to remove the paint had carelessly splashed some of this strong liquid on a part of Old Rollo's anatomy notoriously allergic to turpentine, to which he had reacted most violently, snorting and kicking viciously in his stall. Even now Old Rollo was restive and skittish, his feelings still deeply hurt at the incredible stupidity of those hired hands!

He Pat declared that when he finally had "the goods on us" we would be expelled forthwith, and, furthermore, our fathers would be billed for the cost of Old Rollo's turpentine bath and especially for the hire of the livery stable horse he was compelled to use on his afternoon drives until Old Rollo became, as he expressed it, "presentable" again.

Finally having—as he hoped—"softened us up" with this frightening preamble, He Pat got around to the disappearance of Smith. I remember he shook a gnarled finger in the face of the one of us who would some day be an able college president himself and declared that the police were not going to dilly-dally with us much longer. We'd better tell him—and tell him now—what we knew about the death of Smith and where the body was. They had dragged the cistern just back of what is now White Hall and uncovered a freshly filled "sewer ditch" on Euclid Avenue without success. In vain we protested that none of us had ever heard of Smith until his disappearance, that, while we were in the group under the arc light that night, we were only indulging in the time-honored practice of hair clipping—something all of us had experienced ourselves when we were freshmen. We assured him that nobody had been hurt, nobody had thrown a brick, nobody had been mistreated.

Most fortunately for us, two days later an Associated Press dispatch came out stating that Willis E. Smith had been discovered—alive and well—in Cincinnati. He had related a harrowing story of how, as he was walking through the Southern Railroad yards from Mrs. Beauchamp's to the campus, he had been seized by two hoboes who had dragged him into an empty boxcar and taken him all the way to Dayton before he was released. Then the next day, under police pressure, he confessed that the kidnapping tale was a hoax. The truth was, he said, he disliked college intensely but was afraid to tell his brother. Therefore he had slipped over to the yards, hopped a freight train, and had come to Cincinnati and got himself a job!

Thus ended the "Mysterious Disappearance of Willis E. Smith," but nobody ever found out what had triggered the hallucination of the old lady on the porch.

The following June, at Commencement time, eight young men garbed in black carried an ebony-hued casket in the Class Day parade, on the side of which was a placard reading, "The body of Willis E. Smith."

Many years after our graduation, at another Commencement, the "miscreant" who had become a college president and I sat side by side on the platform. Shades of He Pat! The University of Kentucky was giving to each of us something it awards very sparingly—its highest honorary degree! As the seniors marched forward to receive their diplomas, we talked of old times, and my former roommate recited some of the trials and tribulations of his job. He thought there was one boy whom he would be compelled to expel.

Finally, it seemed to me that a slight pomposity had blurred the memory of his own participation in our college escapades, so I laughed and said, "Why, you talk a lot like He Pat." Then I added, "Before you definitely decide to fire this boy, be sure and let me know. I'll gladly make the journey to your campus for your next convocation. In fact, I may come riding up on Old Rollo, if his mane and tail, that you personally sheared off while I was doing some fancy painting, have grown out! I'd like to walk down to the front of the stage in your fine new auditorium and give students and faculty some material and, perhaps, chapter headings for a future biography of their distinguished and dignified president!"

At our next class reunion, when my old chum walked into my office, I inquired, "Well, how is your incorrigible prankster getting along?" "Oh," said he smilingly, "that boy has improved a lot." And he could not help but chuckle a little when I replied, "I'll bet you are the one who has improved a lot by being more tolerant of youthful follies and foibles that do not involve actual turpitude."

CHAPTER TEN

The Gillis

PROFESSOR Ezra L Gillis, who for many years was Registrar at the University of Kentucky, held at various times almost every high office in the American Association of Collegiate Registrars and the Kentucky Association of Collegiate Registrars. He and Mrs. Gillis were born and reared within two miles of

Spring Motor

my native Glensboro, and he taught in the village school near the covered bridge in what was actually a one-room building, though folding doors permitted it to be divided if the number of pupils made this advisable. It was here and from Gillis that I learned my ABC's.

Years later, following a most successful tenure as head of Minerva College, a small school in Mason County where he taught my dear friend Dr. Herman L. Donovan, former President of Eastern State College and now President Emeritus of the University of Kentucky, Professor Gillis joined the faculty of "State College," and he and his delightful family—Mrs. Gillis and their two lovely daughters Cleo and Inis—moved to Lexington. Although I did not realize it then, their coming to the city from which I had on two occasions so ignominiously departed was a very important milestone in my life.

It was about Christmastime when my father said to me, "Son, Professor Gillis now lives in Lexington, and he and Mrs. Gillis say that they will be very happy to have you stay with them if you go back to school there." Still with a heavy heart at leaving my beloved Salt River Valley, I was willing to try it when the college commenced after the holidays. I was warmly received by these friends whom I had known all my life, and I lived in their home until the end of the college year. By that time I had made a number of friends among my classmates and had accepted an invitation from two of them for us to room together when school opened again in September. But I shall always remember with deepest gratitude the hospitality and encouragement extended to me by the Gillis family.

Professor Gillis was an affable, attractive man, and his warm personality, sound judgment, and mastery of his specialty in the field of higher education made him exceedingly popular. A short time after he came to Lexington he became the first Registrar the college ever had, and it was not many years before he instituted a system of record keeping that revolutionized the duties of that office. Today the Gillis technique is used by registrars in many leading universities throughout the country.

However, Professor Gillis' one and only venture into the field of mechanical invention was not so successful. It was while he was teaching at Glensboro that people began to notice that he was spending much of his spare time in the quarters of the local Masonic Lodge, which was upstairs over a vacant store room just opposite Mr. Catlett's blacksmith shop. With him would be one of his close kinsmen, a prosperous farmer named Ben Franklin, my father, and Mr. Catlett. The reason for these conferences was a dark secret, and when my mother attempted to quiz my father about them he was obviously reticent and evasive.

Finally, one day my father and Gillis climbed into a one-horse spring wagon with a stoutly crated object in the back and set out for Lawrenceburg. There, as I later learned, they boarded a train for Lexington and then another one for Cincinnati, taking the crate along in the baggage car.

However, privacy is difficult to maintain in a small village, and news began to leak out that Professor Gillis had invented a marvelous gadget that would save the housewife from many drudgeries, that a rough working model had been constructed in the Masonic Lodge room, and that a full-sized demonstrator was being manufactured in Cincinnati.

It certainly was an exciting day in our little town when the demonstrator arrived and was put on display at the large country store. People came from miles around to see it. The contraption was about four and one-half feet in height, with a framework of sturdy golden oak which supported a compact, heavily nickel-plated cabinet that housed a steel spring and a winding device, as well as slots and grooves into which appropriate attachments could be inserted. A printed, illustrated prospectus describing in detail the wonderful adaptability of this fantastic machine was on hand and was widely distributed. Addressed "To the Ladies," it contained a glowing recital of the motor's many uses. Being before the day of window screens, it would operate a "fly bush," keeping the pestiferous insects away from the table at mealtime. It would churn and rock a cradle.

Then there was a special paragraph, headed "A Boon to Dressmakers," which I've always believed was written by my father. It read in part: "Few women know that the sewing machine is often the cause of troublesome complaints from which they suffer. But such is the case. The constant downward pressure with the feet and lower limbs of the woman while operating the machine causes a continuous strain on the lower abdominal muscles, thereby frequently caus-

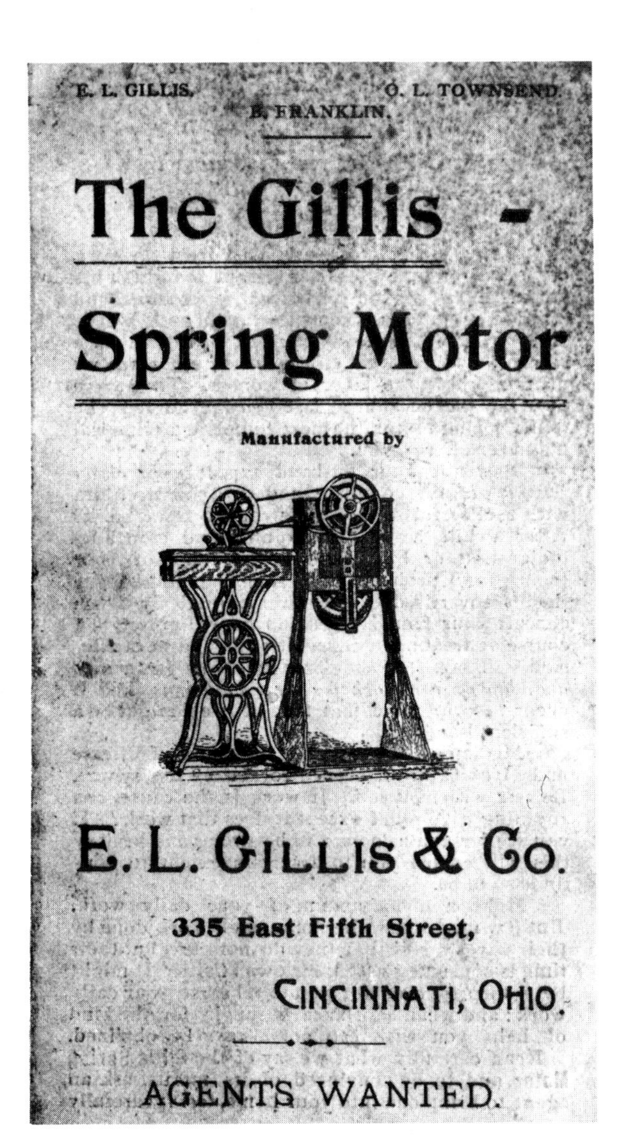

E. L. GILLIS, O. L. TOWNSEND.
B. FRANKLIN.

The Gillis - Spring Motor

Manufactured by

E. L. GILLIS & CO.

335 East Fifth Street,

CINCINNATI, OHIO.

AGENTS WANTED.

PROSPECTUS FOR THE GILLIS SPRING MOTOR (PAGE 1)

TO THE LADIES.

Ladies, is not this a fact that from the very beginning of time man has striven to lighten his labor? Every device, mechanical, agricultural and otherwise, has been invented with this sole aim in view, to lesson the labor of man; but think for a moment and see what efforts have been made by man to lighten the labor of women. They have been few indeed; but at last you are offered The Gillis Spring Motor, the most complete mechanical help ever offered you.

Does not your husband expect your daily routine of work complete, and that you meet him with a cheerful smile on his return from work? After awhile he is disappointed and concludes indigestion or bad blood is the cause of your trouble, and probably buys some patent medicine that is advertised to cure everything. Or if you consult your family physician he will prescribe a course of treatment, collect his bill, and in conclusion will say, *it will become necessary for you to abandon certain work for the time being.* Did it occur to your mind that that of itself might be a sufficient remedy?

Medicine only removes the cause of disease and gives nature a chance to restore the system. Be fair with yourself. If work is the cause, can anything give relief except it does that work? If you are fortunate enough to be strong and healthy this will enable you to a certain extent to continue so to be.

Make a memorandum of your daily work. But few men know the amount of work done by their wives. Not that they do not care, but their time is consumed with their own affairs. It might be a surprise even for you to rehearse your daily work; and when assistance is sought for, the kind of help you wish can not always be obtained.

Read carefully what we say of the **Gillis Spring Motor**, and to be convinced of its merits, ask an agent to bring one into your home, test it carefully

PROSPECTUS FOR THE GILLIS SPRING MOTOR (PAGE 2)

ing prolapsus (falling of the womb), neuralgia, backache, etc. Now we claim that by the use of our motor the tendency to these diseases from this cause is entirely removed, and that the most delicate woman is enabled to operate her most useful sewing machine, with pleasure and profit. Truly this is the woman's friend."

But the disappointment of the inventor and his associates was extremely keen when their precious motor proved to be unequal to the tasks assigned it. The spring was not large enough to keep the "fly bush" moving until the meal was over. It would not rock a cradle until the baby went to sleep; the motive power stopped before the butter was churned. The spring uncoiled before the dressmaker's job was finished, while frequent winding caused early and fatal deterioration and eventual destruction of the spring.

But Professor Gillis, who lived to be over ninety, saw in future years his dream of alleviating the burden of household duties come true from other sources. However, "E. L Gillis & Co." always remembered their youthful, carefree, optimistic ambitious years when they tried so earnestly to promote the public good and, at the same time, establish a successful business for themselves. And thereafter, when Gillis and my father got together and talked over old times and their brief excursion into the domain of invention was mentioned, even after Gillis had become a prominent figure in college circles, it seemed to me that his chuckles were not quite free from nostalgia.

CHAPTER ELEVEN

Two Singers Who

AFTER I HAD BECOME acclimated enough to stay away from Glensboro for a month at a time, nobody ever enjoyed college life more than I did. This was also true of most of the "Old Grads" of my era. The school was small, and everybody

Made a Quartet

knew everybody else. There was close comradeship among students, a flaming college spirit, and intimate contacts—even warm affection—between us and many members of the faculty like Gillis, Noe, Farquhar, McKenzie, Lafferty, Kerr, and Chalkley.

There was little, if any, rush or stress or strain–plenty of time for fun and frolic. No wonder, when these Old Grads meet, either by chance or prearranged reunion, the talk is not about their success in life, nor about scholastic honors, nor much of the serious side of the four youthful years we spent together. On the contrary, the conversation is invariably associated with incidents fondly recalled when someone says: "Do you remember the night . . . ?"

Nor can I forget that on two occasions my life probably was saved by these bull sessions or the anticipation of them. On January 27, 1922, I was in Washington on legal business for the City of Lexington. That afternoon my local co-counsel, who practiced before the government departments, invited me to go with him that evening to a good show at the Knickerbocker Theatre. I reluctantly declined because I had agreed to meet Jesse Miller, "Peg" Moore, and several other U. K. friends for dinner at Harvey's restaurant, where we had reserved a small private dining room. We arrived at Harvey's about 5:30 and, when we came out around midnight, we discovered that a freak snowstorm–unheralded and wholly unsuspected, even by the weatherman–had blown in from Chesapeake Bay, covering the city with a white mantle two feet deep!

Next morning the newspapers were full of the great catastrophe that had occurred when the snow-laden roof of the Knickerbocker had suddenly collapsed, killing nearly one hundred people, including my co-counsel and his wife, and the conductor and other members of his orchestra who had played at Lexington's Ben Ali only a few weeks before.

Twenty years later, when I was legal counsel and a member of the Board of Directors for Southeastern Greyhound Lines, I attended a meeting of the Board in Atlanta. We met all that day in Suite 1212 of the newly renovated Winecoff Hotel. I would have remained over until the following day because I've always disliked spending two consecutive nights on a train; but several of my old classmates were coming to Lexington the next morning, and we planned to be together the rest of the day and during the evening just prior to the afternoon of the Kentucky-Vanderbilt football game.

So after the others were gone I stood at one of the windows of the suite, looking out at the twinkling lights that illuminated the serene atmosphere of this big, peaceful city. Then at 7:40 I checked out to catch the train back to Lexington. Less than three hours later the Winecoff was destroyed by fire, with enormous guest casualties, among them a young family from Lexington, Joe Goodson and his wife and two children, who had stopped there for the night on their way to a Florida vacation.

However, even though night activities of college life always have been an important phase of these bull sessions, not all our adventures were nocturnal. Many happened during broad daylight hours—like the time seven of us went down to Tom Dewhurst's garage, then the only one in town, and rented a big Stanley Steamer with chauffeur to drive to Oxford, Ohio, where our football team was to play Miami University. We folded the cloth top behind the rear seat, fastened on the back a huge blue and white banner with "Kentucky" in large, block letters across it, and set out for Ohio in a gay and festive mood.

I remember the narrow, rough, crooked turnpike between Lexington and Cincinnati which crossed the Southern Railway tracks twenty-three times at grade! There were also at least ten toll gates between Georgetown and the bridge over the river at Covington.

As we entered Scott County somebody suggested that it would be lots of fun, when the gatekeeper came out and raised the pole, to lift our hats or caps, thank him politely, and roll on in a cloud of dust without paying the toll. This we did with much merriment until we reached the last gate at the Ohio River bridge. There, the attendant made no move to lift the barrier, but approached the car with glowering countenance.

"Where you boys think you're goin'?" he inquired in sarcastic, menacing tones.

"Oh," we replied, "we're going to the football game at Oxford."

"No you ain't," he exploded, "you're goin' to jail. They phoned in here from Georgetown and said you jumped the toll gate there. The other toll gate houses don't have phones. How many gates you-all jumped?"

We hesitated a moment before saying, "All of them." Then he really ranted, and we did not extricate ourselves until we paid him not only all the back toll but gave him an extra five dollars to appease his wrath. For the rest of the way our spirits were considerably chastened!

Sometimes certain professors, unintentionally, were the cause of much amusement. One evening William Jennings Bryan, the famous orator, whose popularity remained undimmed despite three defeats for President of the United States, delivered his celebrated lecture on Christ, entitled "The Prince of Peace," at the Lexington Opera House. When it was over I, as president of the college Democratic Club, went backstage, taking with me the vice president, a most vocal and militant member of our organization—who later became a Republican United States Senator—and we invited Mr. Bryan to come out to the campus next afternoon and talk to the young Democrats. The great man received us cordially but said that under his Lyceum contract he was not allowed to discuss politics. He added, however, that he would be happy to come out next morning at chapel hour and talk briefly on some religious subject.

This suggestion was gladly accepted, and the chapel

was crowded to capacity with the entire faculty seated on the long rostrum. The master of ceremonies was Professor James White, acting president, a man of great personal dignity and, due perhaps to the subject he taught as head of the Department of Mathematics, a person of the most precise thought and speech. However, it was evident that on this particular morning he was somewhat ill at ease in the presence of our distinguished guest.

So, following the invocation, Dr. White got up and announced that the program would be opened by Mrs. Dantzler and Professor Farquhar, who would sing a quartet. Well, there was much tittering in the crowd over Dr. White's verbal blunder, of which he seemed wholly unaware, but we could see that it had not escaped Mr. Bryan.

When finally he was presented, the noted speaker beamed warmly upon his audience with that expansive smile which had become a "trademark" of his magnetic personality, and said he had always known that Kentuckians were in a class by themselves. They had the most beautiful women, the fastest horses, and the finest liquor in the world. Their ancestors had killed more Indians than the pioneers of any other region. During the Civil War a handful of Kentucky Confederates could whip a whole regiment of New England Yankees. And yet, in spite of all this, he was quite unprepared to find—even in Kentucky—it took only two to make a quartet!

Of course this brought down the house, and even "Uncle Jimmy" joined in the laughter and applause; but we noticed that his bald head and face, against the background of a fringe of white hair and whiskers, took on a deeply pinkish hue!

CHAPTER TWELVE

Opera Capes and

WHEN I CAME to Lexington public entertainment was nothing like it is today. The fact that we had to devise our own amusements doubtless accounts for many of the escapades that so greatly vexed the college authorities.

There were only two picture shows, and the poor

Empty Pockets

screen reception amply justified their nickname, "flickers." We also had vaudeville at the Hippodrome—called in college boy parlance the "Hipp"—but the real, high-class stage shows were at the Opera House, where Lexington had earned the reputation of being the "best one-night stand in America."

At the Opera House was enacted one scene of an experience still avidly discussed at reunions by those who observed and to an important extent participated in it. One year a roommate of mine, who was a big, good-looking boy—nicknamed "Bull" because of his aggressive line play as regular left tackle on our football team—was madly in love with a beautiful girl from a Northern Kentucky town who also attended school in Lexington.

One day Bull, with obvious anxiety, told me and several other close friends his sweetheart had just informed him that her mother, her brother Percy, and her older sister planned to visit her over the weekend. These folks, whom Bull had never met, were reputed to be quite wealthy and almost austerely "high-toned," and he was terribly concerned about making a good impression. Moreover, he now confessed that, by innuendo and other methods he regarded as subtle, he had given his girl the impression that he was considerably affluent himself.

Naturally, Bull felt that during this visit of those he hoped would some day be his in-laws he must maintain the fiction he had so carefully cultivated. But he had no money! Could he—with unspeakable gratitude—impose upon us sufficiently to borrow all the money we had or could raise and thus avert the disaster that threatened his romance? He needed substantial funds right away, because he wanted to take the entire party to see Olga Nethersole, who on Friday evening was appearing at the Opera House in *Camille*.

So we gave him every cent we had, reserving for ourselves only a quarter apiece to pay for a seat in the second balcony—called the "roost"—for the same show. Then, on that evening, after we had fought our way onto the front row of our high and distant perch and just before the curtain went up, we beheld an impressive sight, which I'm sure was never surpassed in the long history of this fine old, fashionable theatre.

Down the aisle to the dress circle came Bull's party, the women regally gowned and the brother—a distinctly effeminate type—and Bull faultlessly attired in full dress suits. Taking no chances on being outdone by Percy, Bull had gone down to Graves & Cox and rented—as could then be done—evening clothes with all the paraphernalia, including a white vest and ribbed silk opera hat—even a full dress overcoat with a flowing cape lined in white satin! As we witnessed this elegant entrance, there seemed to be no disagreement with somebody's observation: "Well, old Bull sure is getting *our* money's worth!"

Late that evening Bull came back to our room, carefully collapsed his opera hat, parted his long coattails, and sat down in a chair, a perfect picture of proud contentment. "Bill," he said, "I had no idea I would find Percy such a damn fine fellow!"

However, the prospective in-laws, having once tasted my roommate's lavish hospitality, stayed on and on into the next week, wholly unaware of their host's rapidly diminishing financial resources. Finally one night, after I was in bed but not asleep, Bull came in looking extremely disconsolate, slumped down in a chair, and sat there in sad silent reflection. Then he said, "Bill, if that little s.o.b. don't go away tomorrow and take with him that snooty sister and stuck-up mother, I'm sunk. Why," he continued, "that priss, when it comes to buying theatre tickets or picking up a restaurant tab can out-fumble any rookie quarterback I ever saw. He makes belated gestures, but I've never seen him spend a red cent since he's been here."

Being sleepy and somewhat disgusted, I could not resist needling him with the inquiry: "Bull, could you, by any chance, be referring to that 'damn fine fellow' you told me about last week?" Refusing to dignify this crack by reply, Bull merely pulled the brim of his old felt hat further over his eyes and, as I dozed off, he was still sitting there in deep dejection. But the next day Fortune smiled. Percy and his expensive entourage started home, leaving seven or eight college boys extremely happy over their long overdue departure—but absolutely broke!

The old adage "Youth must be served" is very familiar to everybody, but as time goes by I like to recall, with increasing satisfaction, a case where this motto was reversed and youth served elderly years, happily for all concerned.

One September a somewhat reserved and dignified old gentleman came out and, though he was not a candidate for a degree, was permitted to register as a special student in the Law School. We started calling him "Judge," a title he accepted quietly but with obvious satisfaction. We learned—but not from him—that before he had finished the eighth grade he had been compelled to quit school and go to work, and he had worked constantly for sixty years until he retired, well fixed financially, owning several valuable pieces of Main Street business property.

At an early age he had married a good woman, who, however, dominated him, benignly but firmly. It was her settled conviction that, for husbands, the rule should be "All work and no play." Being a recluse herself, she had insisted all these years that our "Judge" should come straight home from work and stay there until next morning. They had no hobbies, no amusements, took no vacations, had no friends who came to call, went nowhere, and had no children.

Shortly after his retirement he had confessed to his wife that his early dream had been to be a lawyer, but he had not been able to gratify that ambition. Then he asked her permission to take some legal subjects at the University, and she gave grudging consent. Soon, of course, he was the pet of the Law College, and he tried pathetically to be "one of the boys." But it was exceedingly difficult to overcome the habits of a long lifetime. He seemed lost, except when actually in the classroom, and would sit in the library, gazing distractedly out the window, apparently much depressed. Moreover, he was very absentminded and found it almost impossible to remember the hours of classes or the days of the week they came on.

Finally, several of us made up our minds that

something drastic had to be done to cheer and loosen him up—and soon. One of my most intimate classmates was George Bain Morrison, called "Bain," a son of Rev. H. C. Morrison, then and for many years president of Asbury, the Methodist college and theological seminary at Wilmore. His maternal grandfather was Colonel George Bain, the famous Chautauqua Circuit temperance lecturer, who was without a peer in his eloquent and scathing denunciation of the "demon rum."

One Thursday afternoon Bain and I decided we needed recreation, so we cut classes and had just left the Law building when we met the "Judge" plodding along, a law book under his arm. "Now is the time we've been looking for," Bain said to me. So we stopped and asked the "Judge" where he was going.

"Why, to corporation class, of course," he replied. Then we said, "Judge, don't you know this is Wednesday. Corporation class is on Thursday." He thought about this for a moment before he shook his head and said, "I thought sure this was Thursday."

By this time we had him by the arm, told him we were going to a show, reminded him he had nothing else to do, and insisted that he come along as our guest, to which, after a little hesitation, he assented. So downtown we went.

We stopped first at the Cafe Royal on South Lime just below Main. We asked him what he'd have to drink, and after some thought he said he had always wanted a mint julep but had just "never got around to it." So we ordered three Old Fitzgerald juleps, which

Equestrian statue of John Hunt Morgan

Cassius M. Clay at the age of 84

were served in tall silver goblets with tender, fragrant mint leaves draped over the frosted sides. After several sips he told us, in guarded tones, as though he might give offense to the bartenders if overheard, that, though having spent his life in Lexington, he had never been in a "saloon" before. He chuckled, however, and volunteered the opinion that being there with us this afternoon was, as he said, "too late to hurt me now."

Suddenly we noticed that the "Judge" was taking a somewhat furtive but very definite interest in the magnificent oil and crayon nudes hanging on the walls. Presently he walked over to a vivid, well executed painting, showing—showing very much indeed—a seductive young female reclining languidly on a couch. Carefully he adjusted his "specs" so that the picture was firmly centered in his bifocals and scrutinized it intently. Then he came back, reached for his julep cup, glanced again at the "lovely lady," and exclaimed in frank astonishment, "Well, I declare!"

The "rootin', tootin' " burlesque show at the Hipp—the first stage performance I'm sure he had ever seen—with its slapstick comedy and scantily attired chorus line, entertained him vastly, so that later, when we told him goodbye at Main and Lime where he caught his streetcar, he said with emotion that made his drooping grey mustache quiver slightly, "You boys have given me the biggest afternoon of my life. I don't envy you anything but your youth. Today will never be forgotten by me." "Ah, Judge," we assured him, "this is just the beginning." And it was!

CHAPTER THIRTEEN

Wildcats and the

I HAVE ALWAYS been profoundly thankful that I was born and reared in a hilly section of the country instead of on the western plains, the deadly monotony of which is so obviously apparent. However, I learned that I had never seen real hills, much less mountains, until the speakers bureau of the State Demo-

Terrified Client

cratic Committee sent me to Eastern Kentucky during Woodrow Wilson's second campaign for President.

I got off the train at Mt. Sterling, where Ryland Musick, a Jackson lawyer, district chairman for Menifee, Wolfe, Breathitt, Magoffin, and Morgan counties, met me. We then went from Mt. Sterling to Frenchburg, some twenty or more miles, in a one-horse spring wagon. I was, in the very beginning, utterly appalled at the fact that east of Montgomery County there was nowhere in all that region an improved road, not one with even the roughest macadam on it. Vehicular traffic was almost entirely along dry creek beds or dirt ridge roads; but most of the inhabitants rode muleback over narrow mountain trails, some of them perilously close to high cliffs. Reaching Frenchburg, we got on our mules and started on a ten-day speaking tour over Musick's territory, which carried us, by a necessarily circuitous route, a distance of nearly two hundred miles.

One evening we spoke at Crockettsville, a little town in Breathitt, not far from the Owsley County line. This place had been known for years, even to the metropolitan press, as the home of Ed Callahan, former Sheriff and Democratic "boss," who, with Judge Jim Hargis of Jackson, had been involved in the notorious Hargis-Cockrell feud which caused their county to be widely known as "Bloody Breathitt." Both Hargis and Callahan at one time or another had been charged with complicity in the assassinations of J. B. Marcum, Dr. B. D. Cox, Jim Cockrell, and perhaps others.

Our speaking was held at the Callahan store, a very large general merchandise establishment, and, the weather being mild, it was decided to address the crowd from the porch of the store. Since I intended to read a few planks in our party's platform, I took up a position in front of a big window, through which a bright light shone from a huge oil lamp swinging from the ceiling inside.

Just then Ryland came over and said to me in a low tone: "I believe you ought to move over to the end of the porch where it is darker than it is here." Completely mystified, I inquired why this made any difference. He replied, somewhat hesitatingly, "You're now standing near the spot where Ed Callahan himself was assassinated two or three years ago. I notice quite a number of Republicans out there, and I know a few who are mean and dangerous when full of moonshine. I don't think they'd shoot you, but they might throw some rocks. Standing more in the shadows, you'd be harder to hit!"

Well, this was very disturbing information indeed. Suddenly I became homesick for the serene and peaceful atmosphere of my native Glensboro and wondered —as I have since in moments of severe stress—why in the world I ever left there! About this time, the county chairman, who knew nothing of the foregoing conversation, stepped forward and began introducing me, and there was nothing to do but go ahead as originally arranged. Most fortunately for me, there was no trouble. However, it is not difficult to understand why my speech was delivered with the greatest trepidation and that I carefully avoided all reference to Republican iniquities. On the contrary, I confined myself entirely to warm praise of our noble President!

This visit to Eastern Kentucky enabled me to more keenly visualize the experience of a client of mine who, some years later, also made his first trip to that region. For the last ten years of his life, I was Kentucky counsel for Joseph Wolf of Chicago, who owned the James E. Pepper Distillery on the Old Frankfort pike and had other interests in the state. Wolf, then an elderly and very wealthy man, had been born to Jewish parents in the city of Darmstadt, Germany. While still in his teens he had run away from home, crossed the Atlantic in steerage, and finally landed in Chicago, unable to speak a word of English and without a cent in his pockets.

For about a year he worked at odd jobs, sleeping in a stable on Clark Street, but picking up the language rapidly. Then he got a job selling on commission part of a bankrupt stock of whisky and discovered that he possessed a remarkable talent as a liquor salesman. For years before he acquired the plant on the death of Colonel James E. Pepper, Wolf was the exclusive distributor of Old Pepper and was the author of the celebrated slogan, "Born with Republic," which appears even now on all the bottle labels.

However, Wolf had less interest in and knowledge of country life than any man I ever knew. He was absolutely unacquainted with animals, domestic and otherwise, except the Kentucky saddle horse he rode each morning in Lincoln Park. I think he told me he had never even been to a zoo.

Several years before I began to represent him his former lawyer had persuaded him to buy three thousand acres of cut over timber land because it might have minerals on it. But this attorney had not been able to induce him to visit his property in all the time he had owned it until somebody drilled a free-flowing gas well very near his holdings. Even under these circumstances, Wolf was somewhat loath to venture into what he called the "wilds," especially when informed that two or three days would have to be spent on horseback.

Finally, however, he arrived in Lexington ready and—as he believed—properly equipped for the "great adventure." He had brought along his Lincoln Park attire—derby hat, silk frock coat, moleskin breeches, Cordovan riding boots, and gold-plated spurs!

However, Wolf's already apprehensive spirit took a further dive when, on reaching Frenchburg, he and his lawyer found that no horses were available. Clad in all his finery he had to mount a scrawny, stubborn, forlorn-looking mule—a strange looking creature, the like of which he had never seen before. Further troubles were not long in coming. Briars and dead ends of overhanging limbs gouged deep scratches in the immaculate surface of his beloved boots. After riding all day they had to put up for the night at a mountain cabin that had only one room and a lean-to.

The hospitable host offered Wolf and his lawyer the only bed in the house; but declining this, they stretched out on quilts—none too clean—laid on the bare lean-to floor, Wolf refusing to remove any of his clothes—not even his Cordovans. Then in a little while some drunken mountaineers on their way to a dance began firing their pistols at the roof of the cabin, shooting off some of the shingles! And my future client remained awake all night, staring into the darkness until daylight, literally "trembling in his boots"!

By noon the next day Wolf had seen more than enough of his property, and they started laboriously over the rough, steep "sidling" trails back to Frenchburg. It had turned extremely hot and sultry, and the mountains, instead of being cool, seemed to shut out even the faintest breeze. Riding through dense woods not far from their destination, they came across a farmer who had captured three half-grown wildcats, which were confined in a wire cage of coarse, heavy mesh.

The lawyer was, at once, vastly intrigued by these fierce-looking creatures, and Wolf reluctantly dismounted with him for closer inspection. The farmer said that the country was "full of 'em," and Wolf got the impression that they traveled in packs and, when grown, were about the size of an Eskimo Husky. Even in comparative repose these animals looked mighty dangerous to the city-bred capitalist. But the lawyer had fun. He poked them through the wire with a tobacco stick, and they would lunge at it, green eyes blazing, snapping and snarling, with their long, sharp fangs bared. Finally Wolf managed to pull away his companion, who, however, seemed wholly preoccupied by the incident and continued to talk about it the rest of the way.

It was past supper time when they reached the small frame Frenchburg hotel and found that the only accommodation available was one room with a double bed in it. The night was so uncomfortable that all windows and doors were left wide open. Worn to a frazzle, Wolf was just drifting off to sleep when suddenly his lawyer hopped out of bed, ran out the door and down the stairs, shouting, "Wildcats! Wildcats! Wildcats!" Wolf, of course, had never heard that his bedfellow both walked and talked in his sleep. So, believing the place attacked by one or more packs of these awful denizens of the forest, he also fled down the steps, barefooted, with night shirt flapping. Turning to the right and hiding in a closet under the stairway, he did not see two men on the front porch grab the sleepwalker and wake him up. It was several minutes before the lawyer and others discovered Wolf, hysterical and almost suffocated in the little closet!

Several times during the years I represented him Wolf related this story, always with deep emotion in his voice and tears in his eyes. I do not believe he ever quite forgave his sleep-walking companion for providing the terrifying climax to an experience in the mountain wilds, which already had proven to be an extremely painful adventure!

CHAPTER FOURTEEN

Black

I CANNOT REMEMBER the time when I first heard about Black Bess, the mare that John Hunt Morgan rode during the Civil War. The veterans of the Salt River Valley and the old soldiers of the Bluegrass all talked about her with abiding enthusiasm and deep affection.

Bess

Possessed of blazing speed, great beauty, almost unlimited endurance, a strong, straight back, exceptional intelligence, and a spirited demeanor which reflected her blooded ancestry, Black Bess was remarkably calm and courageous under the heaviest fire. For the general she responded to every wish with prompt and complete obedience. Colonel Dick Morgan, the general's last surviving brother, and other staff officers were fond of relating how their chief—hotly pursued by Yankees—had galloped Black Bess through his mother's house at Second and Mill streets and escaped down a private driveway.

In 1911 the Bluegrass was full of Morgan's men, most of them hale and hearty despite advancing years. That spring a movement was started to erect an equestrian bronze statue of the general on the courthouse lawn near Upper Street. A fund was quickly raised, and a noted Italian sculptor who specialized in statues of mounted military men—many examples of whose work stood in Washington—was engaged for the undertaking, which everybody hoped would be his masterpiece.

Promptly he arrived in Lexington and set up his studio in a stone carriage house on Second Street in the rear of what was later the Lexington College of Music. The renowned artist worked alone, and with perhaps a slight touch of arrogance he announced that this statute would be in complete accord with the strictest military traditions.

At his request he was supplied with several photographs of Morgan, his saddle, and other accouterments. Then inquiry was made about a picture of the "charger" which he had ridden. He was informed that he could be furnished a picture of Black Bess, the mare that had carried the general through so many perilous adventures. However, at the mere mention of a mare, the sculptor's Latin blood boiled over. He shouted, waved his arms, and reiterated that no statue ever showed a military man riding a mare. This would be inexcusably bad art. He would be ridiculed without mercy by competent members of his profession who knew that generals were invariably mounted on stallions.

However, after it was explained that the veterans and the public generally would never be satisfied with any horse except Black Bess, the sculptor lapsed into sulky silence apparently conceding the point, and it was given no more thought.

The model was finished sooner than expected and there was considerable disappointment at finding that the sculptor had packed and shipped it to the foundry to be cast into bronze before anybody had seen it. The reason he gave was that other commitments were pressing upon him so urgently that this work had to be finished at the earliest possible moment.

When, in due time, the statue came back in permanent form, the sculptor personally supervised the mounting of the canvas-swathed figures on the granite base previously prepared, and then the night before the unveiling he completely draped them with large Confederate flags.

The ceremonies for next day were eagerly awaited by the old soldiers, their kinsmen, and thousands of others in the Bluegrass. Many dignitaries occupied a temporary platform erected nearby—the national and state commanders of the United Confederate Veterans, high officials of the Sons and Daughters of the Confederacy, the Governor of Kentucky, and both United States Senators. Upper Street from Short to Main, Main Street from Upper to Cheapside, and all available space around the courthouse were packed with a dense throng of enthusiastic spectators.

Presently the dramatic moment arrived. The band played "My Old Kentucky Home," then struck up "Dixie." And the beloved "Stars and Bars," by ingenious arrangement of the sculptor, slowly and majestically began to roll down from the top toward the base. The crowd broke into thunderous applause, mingled with the "Rebel Yell" as the head and shoulders of horse and rider were exposed to view—the general, plumed hat in hand as though acknowledging the tumultuous tribute; Black Bess with flowing mane, flaring nostrils, arched neck, shapely head, and those cocked ears which indicated her unceasing alertness the veterans remembered so vividly.

Then, an instant later as the flag dropped lower, the mood of the vast audience completely changed, and the sultry summer air was filled with cries of dismay and indignation. Incredible as it might seem, the sculptor had transformed Black Bess into a stallion. The veterans almost frothed at the mouth with an anger that defied adequate description. Soon, although the dampened ceremonies were not over, small groups began to detach themselves from the audience. They were looking for the sculptor, who had hastily scrambled from the rear of the platform and disappeared.

But the search for this "atrocious desecrator"—this "perfidious creature"—continued. Hearing that he was leaving on the C. & O., which would pull into Lexington shortly, a part of the crowd rushed to the Union Station only to find out later that police officers had taken the bewildered and cringing culprit to Winchester, and he had caught the train there.

More than fifty years have passed since that eventful and shocking day. The tragic alteration of Morgan's mare has been poignantly related in prose and ballad, to be preserved forever in the folklore of America. But Bess herself still prances proudly on her granite pedestal with unabashed equanimity, heedless of the atrocious anatomical outrage inflicted upon her when Art triumphed over Truth!

CHAPTER FIFTEEN

Courtroom

CHARLES KERR, for more than a decade Judge of the Fayette Circuit Court, later Federal Judge of the Panama Canal Zone, was one of the ablest jurists Kentucky ever had. His decisions rarely were reversed by the Court of Appeals. He had been my Corporation teacher in the Law School, and we became

Episodes

life-long friends. Possessed of a sparkling wit, he was in great demand as a toastmaster and afterdinner speaker. Usually he kept this sense of humor under tight rein while on the bench, but occasionally it was difficult for him to do this.

On one occasion a jury was being selected in a

murder case. Under the law these jurors had to be kept continuously together in custody of the Sheriff, both day and night—not only during the trial but until a verdict was reached and they were discharged by the court. For this reason it was Judge Kerr's custom to inquire of each prospective juror whether there was any reason—such as ill health, sickness in the family, or any urgent business matter which would cause a hardship to him if he were required to serve on a murder panel.

On this particular morning, the twelve men having been seated in the jury box, the judge asked his usual questions as to the existence of any reason why any of the jurors should be excused from duty. A young farmer held up his hand. This was his first courtroom experience in any capacity, and it was apparent from his diffidence and self-consciousness that the importance of his position weighed heavily upon him. His wife was almost at the point of childbirth; but he hesitated to mention such a delicate subject to His Honor, especially in the crowded court room! Ordinarily, in speaking of such a situation, he would have used the word "confined," a term quite commonly heard among the country folks.

However, the dignified and formal atmosphere which surrounded him required his predicament to be expressed in his very best vocabulary, and he undertook to use a word which he thought meant the same thing as "confined"; so he said, "Judge, my wife is about to conceive." Judge Kerr managed to keep a straight face as he pounded his gavel and stilled the subdued mirth that rippled through the audience; but it broke out again beyond all control when His Honor replied, with a twinkle in his eyes, "Hurry home at once, young man; if there was ever a time when the husband should be there it is now!"

During the very early years of my law practice, among my few clients was a Vine Street poultry dealer. One day he came in and said that he had shipped by express over one of the railroads fifteen or more crates of young turkeys to a purchaser who lived within a hundred miles of Lexington. He said that because of the dilatory operation of the train they arrived at their destination much later than expected and greatly reduced in weight, and that he had thereby sustained considerable financial loss.

When I presented his claim to the railroad's attorney it was summarily rejected, and I reluctantly filed a suit for my client in the Fayette Circuit Court. The defendant's counsel was a distinguished lawyer, widely known for his legal ability, the stately reserve and scholarly solemnity of his personality, and the ominous gravity with which he tried his cases. Realizing this, I could not help but feel most inadequate, and certainly insignificant, as I faced a contest with such a formidable adversary.

After most of the morning had been consumed by the introduction of testimony for both sides, counsel for the railroad began his argument to the jury. He had been speaking only a few minutes when Judge

Kerr motioned me to the bench. Then, in undertones, he told me that when the time came for me to make my argument he wanted me to tell the jury a certain anecdote which he related in detail.

So when I got up to speak for the poultry dealer and, after reminding the jury that the only question at issue was whether the tardiness of the carrier had been responsible for my client's damages, I said that the inefficient operation of this railroad—the very thing of which we complained—was so habitual and notorious that many stories and legends had long been in circulation about it.

At this point, I related the tale just as His Honor had told it to me. One day a young man and his wife got on the defendant's train for a visit to relatives who lived about seventy-five miles away. The train chugged along at a snail's pace. It stopped at every station and, it seemed, at almost every pig path. It stood on side tracks for long periods of time, yielding the right of way to both passenger and freight trains going in the opposite direction. It backed up and, with great deliberation, took on coal and water.

Finally, the young husband jumped up and pulled the bell cord violently, which brought the conductor hurriedly into the coach where the couple sat.

"My wife is about to have a baby," the husband exclaimed excitedly.

"Well, why did you let her get on here in that fix?" sourly demanded the conductor.

"Oh," replied the husband, "she wasn't even pregnant when we got on here!"

By this time the counsel for the defendant was on his feet, his face flushed with indignation.

"I object, Your Honor," he almost shouted. "This young man is making a highly improper argument."

The judge peered over the half-lenses of his reading glasses. "I'm sorry," he said, "but I was examining the pleadings in the next case to be called and I did not hear what Mr. Townsend said. Will you please state the grounds of your objections?"

Well, it has always been a mystery to me how Judge Kerr managed to maintain his composure while the attorney for the railroad, with mounting wrath, related to him the very same story His Honor had told me not more than fifteen minutes earlier.

When counsel had finished, the judge said in his most judicial manner, "As you know, our courts have held that attorneys, in their arguments to juries, are allowed considerable latitude in the expression of personal opinions and in the use of anecdotes which jurors realize are merely illustrative of counsel's contentions. I do not understand that Mr. Townsend claims that this incident or any part of it actually occurred. I'll have to overrule your objection."

Next day as I was passing his insurance office, Mr. Phelphs, an elderly gentleman who had apparently taken an interest in me and sent me clients, and who had been on the jury, called to me. When I went in he said in his kindly way, "Townsend, would you like to know why you lost your case yesterday?"

"Indeed I would, Mr. Phelphs," I replied. "I thought we had established our claim."

"Well," said he, "you may not have noticed it, but most of the jurors were about the same age as the defendant's attorney, and when we got in the jury room some of them, especially the foreman, talked about what they thought was your discourtesy toward a dignified lawyer who was practicing before you were born. They talked very little about the testimony. The first ballot stood six to six, but finally three more came over to the railroad's side, and by a vote of nine to three a verdict was returned against your client."

I thanked Mr. Phelphs and went out, pondering what he had told me; and from that day to this I've never told another story to a jury.

However, I remember one ludicrous courtroom incident where Judge Kerr's sense of humor was in no way involved. During the years he was on the bench he was fortunate in having a brilliant, eloquent Commonwealth's Attorney, referred to in everyday parlance as the "Prosecutor." He was extremely popular with everybody and especially kind and considerate to young lawyers. He was their idol, and I shall always warmly cherish his memory.

But at the trial table, duty took priority over friendship and, being a master strategist and a genius at cross-examination, he was a terror to defendants if he believed them guilty. On such occasions, when physical assault was presented as a defense, he had a particular technique which he used with a devastating skill.

If the person on trial claimed that the trouble began when his antagonist laid violent hands upon him, causing him to believe that his life was in danger or that serious bodily harm was about to be inflicted upon him, this, if true, was self defense, and he was entitled to acquittal.

But when the Prosecutor's time came for cross-examination, the defendant's case, even before he realized it, took a distinct turn for the worst. At this point the Prosecutor's manner was mild and even ingratiating as he asked his first question: "You say you thought you were in danger of being badly hurt?"

"Yes, Sir, I sure did," the defendant would say.

"Then would you mind stepping down from your chair and demonstrating on me what made you think this?"

Instantly the defendant found himself at a great disadvantage. Whether he was white or colored, he was so impressed by the Prosecutor's appearance and reputation that he already stood in great awe of him. So, invariably, all he could bring himself to do was to shove the Prosecutor gently, tap him lightly on the shoulder, or make some other innocuous maneuver which completely destroyed his direct testimony.

When the Prosecutor got up to make the final speech to the jury he emphasized with deadly effect the defendant's feeble demonstration. Did the jury believe for a moment that what the defendant actually had shown them was sufficient to justify the crime with which he was charged? Of course, the jury in most instances did not, and a verdict of guilty was usually quite promptly returned.

All this had been observed by a certain young lawyer, and he had helplessly watched his own clients suffer from it on several occasions. Then when "Pete" McGee, a stockily built colored man, killed another Negro in an argument over a crap game, this young lawyer was employed to represent Pete. After a careful investigation that uncovered several vital circumstances unfavorable to the defendant, his attorney, with Pete's consent, went to the Prosecutor privately and offered to plead guilty to manslaughter—an offence much less serious than murder—in return for a light prison sentence. "No, sir," replied the Prosecutor, with an asperity unusual with him. "There has been much lawlessness down there, and I intend to break it up by demanding the death sentence in this case."

There being no alternative, counsel for defendant undertook to prepare his case for trial. He emphasized to Pete that the Prosecutor almost certainly would call upon him to demonstrate just what the deceased had done to him before the shooting. He warned Pete: "Remember, your life is at stake and everything depends on showing the jury exactly what the deceased was doing to you just before you shot him. You must forget who you are, who the Prosecutor is, your surroundings, and concentrate on letting the jury know what occurred immediately before the killing."

When the day came for the trial Judge Kerr called the case, both sides announced ready, a jury was quickly selected, and the trial began. Sure enough, the Prosecutor called for the usual demonstration, but he was wholly unprepared for what happened. Like a flash Pete leaped from the witness box and wrapped both of his big hands tightly around the Prosecutor's neck. Completely taken by surprise, the attorney for the Commonwealth jumped back, tripped on a spittoon, and fell sprawling on the floor with the defendant on top of him.

Of course, the members of the jury almost collapsed in their seats with laughter, as did the other spectators, and everybody became positively hysterical when the Prosecutor exclaimed with towering indignation, "Get off me, you damn scoundrel."

When the commotion had subsided and order had been restored, Judge Kerr directed the jurors to retire and consider their verdict. A few minutes later they returned with a finding of acquittal. Pete—and he alone—had won his own case!

The next day the Prosecutor met the young lawyer on the street. His usual good temper had returned, but he shook his finger at defendant's counsel and said with a smile that was a little grim, "You put the defendant up to that, but don't you ever do it again." However, assurance was unnecessary, because, although the Prosecutor remained in office many years after this, he never again called upon a defendant for a personal demonstration of how the fracas started.

CHAPTER SIXTEEN

The Old Lion

PONDERING THE PAST, as one will do with advancing years, I realize now how remarkably free our Valley was from either family or individual enmities or caustic criticism of people.

I remember only a single exception, a then aged man who lived near the Kentucky River quite some

of White Hall

distance away, and who was called the "Old Lion of White Hall," when he was called anything that could be printed. In our community, still strongly Confederate and proslavery though the Negro had been free for many years, the older generation spoke of Cassius M. Clay as if he were a devil with horns and forked tail! It was a long time after I came to Lexington before I had an opportunity to study his career.

From this investigation I found to my surprise that, while by no means free of faults, Clay was one of the most courageous characters, and certainly the most colorful, the state of Kentucky ever produced. Cassius, called "Cash" by those who knew him well, was Henry Clay's cousin. He was tall, big boned, broad shouldered, lean but powerfully built, with a rich, sonorous voice which resembled that of his distinguished kinsman. In an era when foreign travelers, like Michaux, noted that rough and tumble hand-to-hand fighting was almost regarded as a sport in Kentucky, Cash had the agility and flaming impetuosity of a wildcat, and the bowie knife was his favorite weapon.

While at Yale College he came under the influence of William Lloyd Garrison, and, although his mentor was unable to convert him to abolitionism, he did return home after his graduation and join that small group of gradual emancipationists who had so long been intimidated by the aggressive slave power.

When he inherited from his wealthy father a large batch of slaves worth $1,000 apiece he freed them all, saying, "Since I would not be a slave, I will not own a slave." Of course it was not long before his ardent espousal of this unpopular cause provoked heated controversy and eventual bloodshed.

Being a young man of independent means, Cash made up his mind to publish a newspaper, called *The*

True American, which would be largely devoted to the cause of gradual emancipation. He was not unmindful of the experience of James G. Birney, who, having attempted to start an antislavery newspaper at Danville, a town not far from Lexington, was threatened with murder and banished from Kentucky. There were many who warned Clay of a similar fate.

However, in spite of the misgivings of friends and the vicious militancy of the slavocracy, Cash calmly and cautiously set about his task. He selected for his printing establishment the second story of a sturdy brick building near the corner of Main and Mill streets in Lexington. He securely barred the first floor windows and lined the outside doors with heavy sheetiron.

The only approach to the several second story rooms, a steep, narrow stairway, was guarded by two brass four-pounder cannon loaded with Minie balls and nails and mounted so that they would rake the first landing breast high. Then he instructed his staff that if the worst came to pass, that if a mob, having sledged through the doors and having survived the hail of lead and nails, was about to invade the printing offices, they were to escape through a hatchway in the roof, while he remained behind to blow up the place with three barrels of gunpowder secreted in one corner of the composing room!

However, when the war with Mexico broke out Clay dropped his feud with the slave power, and the local military company known as the Lexington Light

Infantry assembled in the courthouse yard unanimously elected him as their captain. At the end of the war he had won the admiration of his men, and his conduct had been so exemplary that—his extremely unpopular views on slavery temporarily forgotten—he was tendered a grand reception in Lexington. Abraham Lincoln's father-in-law, Robert S. Todd, delivered the address of welcome, and Clay was presented with a jeweled sword.

Unfortunately, this truce was short lived. The bitter slavery advocates entered into a conspiracy to assassinate Clay and enlisted the services of Samuel M. Brown, a fearless, quick tempered, dangerous man, who boasted that "out of forty fights" he had "never lost a battle." The deed was to be done at a proslavery meeting at Russell's Cave near Lexington, because Clay would almost certainly be there to interrupt the speaker.

Their surmise was correct, and, when the interruption came, Brown rushed him in front while one of his co-conspirators struck him a heavy blow on the head with a club, numbing an arm and dazing him momentarily.

"Clear the way and let me kill the damn rascal," ordered Brown.

The crowd fell back. Clay found himself in an open space—Brown standing some fifteen feet away with a "six-barrelled" pistol leveled at his breast.

Forced to run or be shot, Clay chose not to run. Drawing his bowie knife, he advanced upon his adversary. Brown waited until his intended victim was almost within arm's reach and then fired. Distinctly feeling the shock of the bullet and realizing that he could be shot five more times in quick succession, Clay closed on Brown before he could shoot again and with fierce thrusts of his knife laid his enemy's skull open to the bone, cut off an ear, and dug out an eye. In another instant the proud hero of forty fights was thrown over a low stone wall and rolled ignominiously down the bluff into the dark waters of Russell's Cave. Clay was immediately rushed by his friends into a nearby house and stripped to the waist in search of his wounds. To their amazement it was discovered that the ball from Brown's pistol had struck the silver-lined scabbard of the bowie knife and, being deflected, had lodged harmlessly in the back of Clay's coat, leaving only a red spot over the heart.

Among other physical encounters during these exciting days was the tragedy at Foxtown, a village on the Lexington-Richmond turnpike. A debate between Clay and Squire Turner soon turned into a brawl between Clay and Turner and his three sons, Alfred, Cyrus, and Thomas. It ended when Clay disemboweled Cyrus and was himself almost fatally wounded by the Turners.

It was about this time that Clay invented and had a Cincinnati silversmith make for him the wickedest looking knife that anybody in Kentucky had ever seen or heard of. It had a seven inch, razor sharp blade.

Strapped securely but loosely under the left arm, it hung from its scabbard of coin silver—unlike all other knives—handle down, the blade held in place by a spring at the hilt.

"A grasp of the handle will trip the spring and release the long, curved, double-edged blade at belly level," said Clay in explaining its wonderful simplicity and efficiency of operation. "No assailant will ever be looking for a weapon drawn from that position," said he. "Therefore, as a foe advances, all one has to do is to point the blade at his navel and thrust vigorously."

The passage of the Kansas-Nebraska Bill by Congress and Clay's scathing denunciation of it made him in great demand as a speaker in the North and East. He was even invited to speak in Springfield, Illinois, though when he got there he found the State House doors closed against him. The meeting was then moved to a grove where the State Capitol stands today.

Lincoln, who had known him since the long vacation days spent in Lexington with his wife's family, called on him when he arrived and was present at the speaking, but did not sit on the platform. He lay on the turf whittling sticks, Clay recalled in later years, and he added, "I shall never forget his long, ungainly form, and his ever sad and homely face."

During the speaking, a loud voice shouted from the audience: "Would you help a runaway slave?" Clay destroyed the heckler by the quick retort, "That would depend on which way he was running."

Long after the crowd had dispersed that afternoon Lincoln and Clay sat in the shade and whittled and talked about slavery. Clay says in his *Memoirs*: "Lincoln was then but little known to the world, but I flatter myself, when he listened to my appeal for universal liberty for more than two hours, that I sowed good seed in good ground, which in the providence of God, produced in time good fruit."

It was about this time that Lucretia Mott of Cleveland gave a dinner in Clay's honor. Both white and colored emancipationists were guests. When the time for toasts arrived, a colored leader stood up and enthusiastically proposed: "Here's to Cassius M. Clay, the liberator. Though he has a white skin, he has a black heart." Clay remembered that it was a long time before his friends ceased to twit him about this dubious compliment.

By national convention time of 1860, Clay was one of the most widely known men in the United States and was generally popular, except in slave territory. After Lincoln's nomination for President, Murat Halstead, in his newspaper articles concerning the Chicago Convention, wrote that if the delegates on the floor could have nominated Clay for Vice President he would have been chosen by acclamation, and that at one time a thousand voices shouted, "Clay! Clay!" But finally, for "geographical" reasons, Hannibal Hamlin was nominated, though Clay received 101 votes.

Clay campaigned vigorously for Lincoln, and during

the first ten days after his inauguration, when Washington was almost wholly undefended from treason within and assault from without, Clay organized and armed a band of doughty, rollicking young adventurers called the "Clay Battalion," and guarded the White House and the Navy yard.

After the immediate peril was over the President issued an order thanking Clay for his services. Calling him to the White House, Lincoln presented him with a Colt's revolver as a testimonial of his regards.

A short time after Lincoln became President he appointed Clay United States Minister to Russia. He and Mrs. Clay took up residence in the American Embassy at St. Petersburg; but in a few months Mrs. Clay came back home and never returned to Russia, claiming that the winters there were too severe. In 1862 Clay paid a brief visit to the United States, and Lincoln commissioned him a Major General of Volunteers. But in a little while he resumed his duties in Russia and remained there until the late sixties, when he resigned, returned to Kentucky, and occupied an elegant mansion on his plantation of twenty-two hundred acres, called "White Hall," near the Kentucky River.

Here he found himself in an atmosphere of extreme hostility. Plantation owners held him personally responsible for the loss of their slaves. His friends in the Republican Party left him when he came out for Horace

Greeley, Democratic candidate for President. The Ku Klux Klan—then rampant in Kentucky—denounced and threatened him when he armed the Negroes and marched them to the polls to vote.

But the heaviest blow fell when a Russian boy, whom he acknowledged as his son, came from St. Petersburg to live at White Hall. Promptly Mrs. Clay left him and moved to Lexington with her children, where she obtained a divorce. One misfortune followed another in quick succession. The Kluxers burned his barn, stole his livestock, and scared off his servants. With Lincoln's pistol he had to kill Perry White who attempted to assassinate him.

The Russian boy, who went by the name of Launey Clay, grew up shiftless and dissolute. He would disappear for months at a time, leaving the "Old Lion of White Hall," as Clay—with his shaggy white hair and full beard—came to be called, completely alone in his big, empty house. At times, on long summer evenings—hungry for some contact with life in any form—he would open his unscreened windows so that he might watch the bats flutter in and pick the flies off the walls!

It was about this time that people began to hear that the Old Lion, who was eighty-four, was going to marry Dora Richardson, the fifteen-year-old sister of one of his tobacco tenants. There was tremendous indignation and excitement about this, so much so that on November 14, 1894, the day of the wedding, the

Lexington morning newspaper sent its reporter over to White Hall. Here is his vivid narrative of an exceedingly strange event:

"The second childhood of Cassius Marcellus Clay, if such be his present state, does not prevent him from being a conspicuous figure of American history. While in his younger years, he was a veritable gladiator in the exciting arena of abolition, while in his mature years he served his country in the halls of St. Petersburg as the American representative to that mighty nation, he is far happier today than he was receiving the plaudits of four million slaves whose shackles he had helped to loosen, or listening to the adulation of the courtiers in the American Legation at Russia's capital.

"When I arrived at White Hall yesterday morning at about 9 o'clock, after a long, cold buggy ride over the hills and through the valleys bordering on the Kentucky River, I was met at the front door, which is of beautifully carved wild cherry with knobs of solid coin silver, by a handsome dark complexion, spare-built young man of medium height who politely inquired who I was. And upon being told that I was a newspaper reporter and recognizing me from a previous visit some time ago, he conducted me down the wide hall to the library.

"As we entered the large, richly furnished room with shelves along one entire side, running to the ceiling and filled with books, with portraits in heavy gold frames and rare tapestries hanging on each of the other three sides, the old General was busily replenishing the wood which snapped and blazed cheerfully from the big fireplace. Laying down his poker, I was greeted by this white-haired old man with as much cordiality as was ever extended a royal visitor.

" 'You have met my son Launey,' said he to the young man who stood beside him. Nodding my head, I thought it was about time to explain my intrusion, so I quickly stated to the General that the American people, through me, their reporter and representative, desired to attend this wedding, which I understood was to take place that morning. I waited with my heart in my mouth as the old man hesitated a moment, but I immediately relaxed when he smiled and said, 'Well, I will say to you what Blaine said to the committee who waited on him and asked him if he would receive the people who wanted to see him. Blaine replied and said that if the people wanted to see him, he supposed he would have to see the people. If the people, after all these years, have that much interest in me, then I will have to be accommodating.'

"So saying, the General walked over to a large walnut chest and brought old Bourbon out. While he mixed himself a light toddy (despite other excesses, Cassius Clay has always been a most temperate user of alcohol) your reporter took a heavy straight, thereby stopping in their tracks the chills and shivers running over him from his twenty-three mile ride.

"Mr. Clay said that his children, meaning his children by Mary Jane Warfield Clay, had placed every possible obstacle in the way of his marriage. He said, 'They persuaded my old friend Judge John Chenault not to marry me. I then asked Squire Green B. Million but he refused. Yesterday I suspected my former friends and relatives might get an injunction restraining me from marrying Miss Richardson. They thought they had me caught like a rat in a trap.

" 'So,' he continued, 'I determined to thwart their designs, and, after dark last night, I armed McClellan Richardson, a brother of Dora, and Barlow Clark, one of my farm hands, and sent them eighteen miles into the foothills to Squire Isaac Newton Douglas, who is a good Christian, a kind-hearted gentleman, and one who sympathizes with me in my troubles. The Squire got up out of bed and rode all night over the roughest dirt roads and trails so that he might get here this morning. He has just finished washing up and scraping off the mud and is now having a bite of breakfast in the kitchen. When he is ready, the ceremony will then take place.'

"In a few minutes Squire Douglas, a tall, slightly stooped mountaineer in butternut, hand woven jeans, a man of a good deal of natural, simple dignity, came from the direction of the kitchen into the room. With him was Doctor Smith, a physician of Richmond, a collateral relative of the General's, and McClellan Richardson, a sturdy man about thirty years of age, obviously of the tenant class. Upon their arrival the old General disappeared through the dining room door and immediately returned, leading pridefully his bride-elect by the hand.

"Several months past fifteen years of age, Dora Richardson, daughter of a deceased sawmill worker at nearby Valley View, tall for her age and decidedly mature in physical appearance, hardly looks the child she is. She wore no gloves, no orange blossoms, and carried no bride's roses in her hands. She has a pleasant, rather striking face, but her cheek bones are too prominent for real beauty, and she is altogether rustic in her appearance and manner.

"The scene was a touching one, never before and probably never again to be equaled in American life. The strangely paired couple stood quietly expectant as the Squire thumbed awkwardly through his battered prayer book. A huge stick of wood burned in two, and the fire flared a little, lighting up the fine bindings of the books, the gilded picture frames, and especially the exquisite copper engravings, Grand Duke Alexis and his beautiful Princess, warmly inscribed by each of them had presented to General Clay on their own wedding day, at which he was an honored guest. Upon the death of Alexander II, which occurred quite a while ago, the Grand Duke had become Alexander III, Emperor of Russia, and his Princess the Empress.

"Yesterday across the thousands of miles of land and sea according to the *Cincinnati Enquirer*, which I carried in my overcoat pocket, the dead body of General Clay's royal friend was passing through the densely crowded streets of St. Petersburg to the Cathedral of Lavadia, where his funeral was to be held with great pomp and ceremony. And his death, which I have since learned from the *Telegraph,* vies with General Clay's marriage on the front pages of this morning's metropolitan newspapers.

"The ceremony began, and the man who had led thousands to victory in a crusade for human liberty, who had joyously faced death in innumerable desperate and personal encounters, who in his youth was a perfect Apollo in appearance, if not a Napoleon in the cause of freedom, whose portrait then hung in the palace of a dead Emperor, stood as meekly as a little child with an expression of unspeakable happiness upon his time-worn but still fresh and almost youthful features. By his side stood that simple country girl, as shy as a gazelle, knowing as little of the great world in which her venerable husband had played so conspicuous a part as the most untutored daughter of nature.

"The ceremony was very brief and, when it was over, the General gave her a vigorous kiss which she bashfully but willingly returned. In another moment, she had disappeared through the dining room door, and Dr. Smith and I sat down before the fire, listening with rapt interest to the General's reminiscences of his days in Russia, which came floating back upon him when I showed him the newspaper account of the Emperor's funeral.

"He is in excellent health, erect and muscular as an Indian, and bids fair to live many years if he will only quit fighting. He walked with me to the door, talking in his agreeable and courtly way. My rather hefty hand was lost and helpless in the grasp of that enormous paw—now so gentle—which had laid such violent hold upon so many luckless adversaries. Some think the old General is crazy, but I do not think so. His mind is as clear as a bell. I do not even think he is in his second childhood. But if he is, I shall, hereafter, have no fear of growing old."

As Judge Logan, Lincoln's law partner, used to say, there was a great "upscuttel" in Richmond and Lexington over this "outrage." The officials thought that this old "cradle snatcher" must be promptly taken into custody as a contributor to juvenile delinquency. Knowing well the violent pugnacity of the Old Lion, Judge Chenault concluded that the occasion required the summoning of what was then known as a *posse comitatus*. The sheriff, at the order of the county judge, could be directed to form a committee of the people to put down any disorder that the sheriff's office was unable to cope with. Under the statutes, the county judge was the only one who could issue such order, and, as the statute further provided, the sheriff was required to make a report of the result in writing.

It could not have been more than two or three hours after the reporter had left the house that the sheriff and six of his posse, heavily armed, rode down the lane to White Hall. Hitching their horses and taking proper precautions, they advanced under cover up to the front of the house. The old general had been warned, apparently, of their approach, because he stood waiting for them on the piazza. He had one of his cannon with which he had so valiantly defended his anti-slavery newspaper, the *True American*, out there. He was short of the proper sort of ammunition, but he had done his best; he had loaded it with pieces of trace chains, horseshoe nails, and fragments of old horseshoes. He had his Winchester rifle with him, his bowie knife strapped across his chest, and the revolver that President Lincoln had presented to him.

Nobody knew who fired first, but at least sixteen bullet holes still remain in that front door and the piazza columns. The old general fired his cannon and knocked down the tree the sheriff was behind. He emptied his rifle and then charged down the steps with his pistol in one hand and bowie knife in the other.

The sheriff, in strict obedience to the law, made his written report as follows:

"Richmond, Ky., Wednesday, Nov. 14, 1894. Judge John G. Chenault, Dear Judge: I am reporting about the posse like you said I had to. Judge we went out to White Hall, but we didn't do no good. It was a mistake to go out there with only seven men. Judge, the old General was awful mad. He got to cussing and shooting and we had to shoot back. I thought we hit him two or three times, but don't guess we did—he didn't act like it. We came out right good considering. I'm having some misery from two splinters of wood in my side. Dick Collier was hurt a little when his shirt-tail and britches were shot off by a piece of horseshoe and nails that came out of that old cannon. Have you seen Jack. He wrenched his neck and shoulder when his horse throwed him as we were getting away. Judge, I think you'll have to go to Frankfort to see Brown (John Young Brown who was governor). If he would send Captain Longmeyer up here with two fielders, he could divide his men and send some with the cannon around to the front of the house—but not too close—and the others around through the corn field and up by the cabins and the springhouse to the back porch. I think this might do it. Respectfully, Josiah P. Simmons, High Sheriff."

Nothing further being attempted, the Old Lion and Dora for two and one-half years lived quietly at White Hall. Then she grew homesick for her native Valley View, craved companions of her own age, and her venerable husband gently put her in his buggy and took her back to her humble birthplace—a little shack in a sawmill village on the Kentucky River. In further obedience to her wishes, he gave her a divorce.

The last romantic episode of the Old Lion's long tumultuous life was over. He was alone again at White Hall, reading the classics, tending his flowers and shrubs, feeding the birds, and watching the bats. Those who had known him in the bright noontide of his fame were dead. His children remained estranged. All that the countryside knew of him now or cared to know was that up there on the hill lived an eccentric old man who resented fiercely any invasion of his rights.

One night three denizens of the nearby river cliffs, seeking revenge and valuable silverware brought from Russia, broke into the mansion. The Old Lion was asleep, but he woke up and, with Lincoln's pistol and his bowie knife, fought his last mortal combat. A terrified Negro boy from one of the cabins on the place galloped all the way to Richmond to report the violent "goings on" in the darkness up at the "big house."

Law officers found the Old Lion sitting calmly, meditatively, before flickering embers in the library. Close gunfire had left him with a bullet-punctured bathrobe, scorched and smoking, and several superficial body wounds bleeding slightly. Two of the intruders were dead.

Some months later, however, the General—nearly ninety-three—took to his bed, suffering—sometimes most acutely—from the infirmities of age. But he kept his bowie knife under his pillow. More and more he lived in the eventful, romantic yesteryears. He fought Sam Brown again at Russell's Cave. He whittled and talked about slavery with Lincoln under the tall trees in Mather's pasture. He strolled along the beach of Kronstadt Bay with his friend, the future emperor. On the smoothly frozen Neva River he skated the stately quadrille with beautiful Anna Jean Petroff, star of the Imperial Russian Ballet, mother of his Russian son.

And then, near twilight on the twenty-second day of July, 1903, a devastating tornado suddenly struck the Bluegrass. It unroofed every barn on White Hall plantation. The courthouse cupola and church spires in the nearby town of Richmond were demolished. Over at Lexington china in closets was crushed by concussions which seemed like earthquakes. A bolt of lightning struck the statue of Henry Clay standing on its tall pedestal in the Lexington Cemetery and hurled the head one hundred and forty feet to the ground.

In less than half an hour it was over. The stars came out, the wind sank to a fresh, gentle breeze, the thunder and lightning ceased. Big Jim Bowling, the general's nurse, tiptoed into the sick room to blow out the oil lamp as he usually did before his patient went to sleep. But tonight it was not necessary. He was already asleep, his last sleep. Lying on his back, the handle of his knife peeping out from under the big pillow, his pain-wracked features now untroubled and serene, the restless, violent, stormy spirit of the Old Lion of White Hall had gone fearlessly forth to meet its Maker in the mightiest tempest that Central Kentucky had ever known.

CHAPTER SEVENTEEN

Two Preacher

IT SEEMS STRANGE indeed that one who deserves so little at the hands of the clergy should have had—through long years of happy association—two intimate and devoted friends who were preachers of world renown. Dr. William E. Barton was pastor of the Oak Park Congregational Church, located in a

Lincolnians

beautiful suburb of Chicago. Dr. Edgar DeWitt Jones was pastor of the Woodward Avenue Christian Church in Detroit, said to have the largest Protestant membership in the United States. These men were both much older than I was, Barton being my senior by twenty-five years.

When I first met Barton, he was looking for information about the Rev. Henry Sparrow, half-brother of Lincoln's mother, and his descendants. He had been able to find no record of them in their original county of Mercer since 1827. I informed him that in that year the section of Mercer where the Sparrows lived had been cut off to form a part of the newly organized county of Anderson.

Thereafter I took him many times to see Lincoln's kinsmen in my old home county, going out of our way to pass through Glensboro and up the bridge hill, where he never tired of hearing about "Skip" and the "hant."

Barton was a very handsome man, even in his later years—tall, big boned, slender, erect, with merry blue eyes, ruddy complexion, and a full beard, heavy, snow white, and neatly trimmed in the Vandyke style. He had a delightful sense of humor, but also a natural, wholly unfeigned dignity that went well with his calling.

We made many historical excursions in Kentucky, Indiana, and Illinois, and, in this connection, I am reminded of an incident which only at a later time Dr. Barton came to regard as really amusing. He had just returned from London where he had presided at the sessions of the International Council of Protestant Churches when he got up a party to explore old court records of the Eighth Judicial District where Lincoln had ridden the circuit. Besides Barton, who was just completing his *Life of Abraham Lincoln*, the group consisted of former United States Senator from Indiana, Albert J. Beveridge, just beginning his own Lincoln biography, Henry Horner, noted criminal court judge of Chicago, who later was elected and re-elected Governor of Illinois, owner of a valuable collection of Lincolniana, and Townsend, then writing an article on "Lincoln, the Lawyer" for the *American Bar Association Journal.*

Realizing from previous experience that documents of the Lincoln period usually were stored in dark courthouse attics covered with dull gray dust and frequently coal soot, we provided ourselves with coveralls and an electric lantern. Thus, as we thought, fully equipped, we sallied forth with eager anticipations.

However, after our very first search, we were confronted with a serious situation we had entirely overlooked. The dust and soot were soiling Dr. Barton's immaculate whiskers! At this point, somebody suggested a remedy; so we stopped at a country store and bought half a yard of black calico, and cut out a space large enough for eyes and nose. Then Barton donned this unique beard protector, holding the top in place with his hat and stuffing the bottom under his coveralls, and this device worked perfectly.

So we traveled merrily on, finding many interesting things, until one warm afternoon we reached a little county-seat town down on the Illinois River. We drove up to the back of the courthouse, put on our coveralls, and Barton adjusted his beard protector and picked up our lantern. Then we walked around the building toward the front entrance.

As we turned the corner we observed three men

lounging in the shade of a tree. When they saw us they jumped up, pulled pistols, flashed badges, and demanded that we throw up our hands, which, of course, we promptly did, but we were completely mystified and dumbfounded. We had no way of knowing that only that morning four convicts had escaped from the penitentiary at Joliet!

The sheriff and his two deputies advanced upon us, and one deputy grabbed the front of Barton's coveralls, jerking the black "mask," as he called it, from our preacher's face, and Barton—completely ignoring the officer's pistol—instantly struck him a smashing blow on the side of the head with the lantern. There is, of course, no telling what might have happened if the sheriff, at this time, had not seized Judge Horner—who had kept his back turned to hide his amusement at our preacher's predicament—and swung him around, only to fall back with profound and incoherent apology as he recognized, from newspaper pictures, that the person he was manhandling was the distinguished jurist from Cook County!

Well, explanations were made and regrets expressed all around, but it was some little bit before Dr. Barton became his usual genial self and we dared mention the fact that our damaged lantern needed repairs.

In the autumn of 1930, while preaching in Boston, Dr. Barton suffered a heart attack and, after a few days, was moved to New York, where his son Bruce could be near him. At the time he was stricken, he was not far from the finish of his two-volume work *President Lincoln*. In one of his letters to me from the hospital he said: "I expect to recover a good deal of vigor and, with God's blessing, to make other Lincoln pilgrimages with you. But, if I should fall by the way, I want you to complete my book and see that it reaches the publishers."

Springtime had come again when I wrote in my preface of *President Lincoln*: "The author of this book laid down his pen at the Second Inaugural and, obedient to his request, I have written the three concluding chapters and have lent such assistance in the final revision of the manuscript as the exacting duties of a law practice have allowed. Of course, these chapters are not what they would have been had the author lived to write them himself. And, doubtless, one may find other shortcomings in the book which would not exist had he made his own revision. As was said of Ulysses, so it may be said of Dr. Barton—'There is none left to bend his bow'."

Dr. Edgar DeWitt Jones was a suave, breezy, eloquent, six-foot-three Texan with a marvelous voice, reputed to be the best pulpit orator in America. On several occasions I took him to Glensboro and showed him the sights. He hugely enjoyed what he called the "Billy goat tale" and had me relate it when we would be together and with others in Detroit, New York or Washington.

When I wrote the introduction for his book *Lincoln*

and the Preachers I told this anecdote about him, in his own words, just as he had given it to me.

"I dreamed I went to the bank in Detroit where I do my business and told the Vice-President I wished to make a loan, considerably larger than any loan I had negotiated hitherto. The banker said, 'We have been making you loans on your own name, but for this sum we'd appreciate you giving us another name also.' 'That is all right,' I replied, 'whose name would you like?' 'Well now,' the banker answered, 'how about Abraham Lincoln—he appears to be a friend of yours?' I said that was agreeable to me, and I set out for Springfield. Mr. Lincoln was sitting in his plain office, looking over some papers. He greeted me cordially and asked what he could do for me. I told him, and he said, 'Let me see the note.' I handed it to him—and just then I woke up! Now, I'll never know whether or not my credit was good with Abraham Lincoln!"

One day Dr. Jones visited Lincoln's tomb in Springfield. As he entered, genial old Herbert Fay, the longtime custodian, was showing a group of Polish tourists, employed at a factory in Hammond, Indiana, the spot where Lincoln and his wife lay beneath a large block of granite. Seeing Dr. Jones, Mr. Fay introduced him as a famous Lincolnian and requested him to say a few words on his favorite subject. Edgar, as usual in such an unexpected situation, fell back on poetry and recited, as only he could, James T. McKay's exquisite sonnet, "The Cenotaph."

"And so they buried Lincoln? Strange and vain!
Has any creature thought of Lincoln hid
In any vault, 'neath any coffin lid,
In all the years since that wild spring of pain?
'Tis false—he never in the grave hath lain.
You could not bury him although you slid
Upon his clay the Cheops pyramid
Or heaped it with the Rocky Mountain chain.
They slew themselves; they but set Lincoln free.
In all the earth his great heart beats as strong,
Shall beat while pulses throb to chivalry
And burn with hate of tyranny and wrong.
Whoever will may find him anywhere
Save in the tomb—not there, he is not there."

Edgar said he noticed an extremely puzzled look on the faces of these tourists as they left but thought nothing particularly of it until, after chatting with Mr. Fay a few minutes, he went outside and found the group waiting for him at the parking place. One of them came up to him and said, "Say, Mister, we don't know who to believe. Just before you come in, the old feller was pointin' at the floor and tellin' us 'He's right down there.' Then you come in and say, 'Aw, naw, he ain't there. You gotta look for him somewhere else'."

It was the doctor's opinion that making the proper explanation, in understandable terms, to these foreign, almost illiterate, but well meaning, truth seeking people, was the hardest job he ever undertook.

CHAPTER EIGHTEEN

The Equestrienne

WHEN A LAWYER has practiced his profession as long as I have, he has at least a few experiences which are vividly retained in memory. One morning a most attractive young woman came into my office. She very modestly introduced herself as the "trick horse rider"—I discovered

Queen and the Barber Lawyer

later that the show posters billed her as the "Equestrienne Queen"—with Ringling Brothers Circus that had arrived in Lexington earlier in the day. She told me this story.

In her very early twenties she started working for Ringling, and a short time later she married an animal trainer, who was considerably her senior. They had a son, and when the son was three years old her husband suddenly disappeared, taking the boy with him. All efforts to find them had proved fruitless for a couple of years, at which time she heard that her husband had just died of a heart attack in Alabama.

Hoping to find some trace of her son, she took the first train down there and went through the dead man's personal effects. Finally she found a snapshot of the boy sitting on the front porch of a small frame cottage. The number 121 was painted under the top step, and the words "Smith Street" were stencilled on the edge of the curbing. This was all—no other clue as to his whereabouts—nothing whatever to indicate the town or city where the house was located.

However, meager as the facts were, she continued the search for her son. Whenever the circus train arrived at its destination she went directly to the Traveller's Aid Bureau and consulted the city directory to see if that particular town had a "121 Smith Street," which most of them did. But none of the houses resembled the one in the picture, and nobody knew anything about the boy.

Today she had followed her usual practice and had found Smith Street in Lexington—about two blocks long—just west of North Broadway, intersecting Fifth Street. Riding in a cab down Fifth near Smith, to her unspeakable joy, she met her little son on his way to school. Getting out of the cab, she ran to him, told him she was his mother, and tried to embrace him—all of which seemed to frighten the little fellow very much, and he hurried off up the street toward the school building.

Then she walked down to 121 Smith Street, where she found an elderly couple—poor, but quite respectable. They were childless and had come to regard the little boy as their very own after his father had left him with them when he was about four years old.

Naturally they were very cool toward what they called that "circus woman," and they remained so even after she had shown them the snapshot and his birth certificate and had stressed the fact that she had no intention of taking the boy away from them. All she wanted was to be recognized as his mother, have an opportunity to see him whenever she could, and be given his legal custody. However, the old folks were positively adamant and finally ordered her out of the house, declaring: "We will fight you in court if necessary."

Under the circumstances there was nothing to do except to ask the court, which luckily was then in session, for a writ of habeas corpus; and thereupon an order was issued requiring the boy to be produced before the judge at eleven o'clock that morning. At the appointed hour the foster parents appeared with the boy and their lawyer. On request of defense counsel the judge, very properly, postponed the hearing for three days. However, my client very much wanted her son to see the circus; and, over the strong protest of the defendants and their attorney, the court ruled that he might attend in my custody, with the understanding that promptly after the afternoon show I would return him to 121 Smith Street.

So we went to the circus. My client had obtained for us two seats in the first row of the reserved center section. And we barely had time to sit down when the band struck up a lively tune, and the "Equestrienne Queen," gorgeously attired in a long-skirted dark green velvet Empress Eugenie costume, wearing a small hat with a large ostrich plume swept back from her lovely face, riding sidesaddle, galloped through the front entrance on the most beautiful Palomino horse I've ever seen. After cantering around the wide oval track she rode back until she was about fifteen feet from us and began to put this remarkable animal through his paces.

At her unobtrusive bidding he, among other things, lay down, hopped on three legs, reared and pranced a few steps on two, and waltzed gracefully to the strains of the "Blue Danube," all of which drew loud applause from the audience.

Only the little boy showed no reaction. He sat quietly and silently beside me, watching the performance intently. As a finale, she rode up close to the railing behind which we sat and had the horse kneel and bow his head, while, with a significance of which the audience was wholly unaware, she smiled and waved her hand in our direction.

As horse and rider left the track I asked the boy if he would like to go out and see his mother, and he nodded assent. We found her back of the big tent. She had dismounted and was leaning against the saddle in tears, believing that the supreme effort of her professional career had wholly failed to impress her son. In an instant, however, her mood completely changed as the little boy rushed into her eager arms, and she radiantly lifted him and put him astride the magnificent Palomino.

Well, this was one experience in the law that had a remarkably happy ending. Upon the trial of the case, my client established beyond question that she was the mother of the child and was awarded his custody; but she never took him away from the foster parents who loved him dearly and to whom he was deeply devoted.

Knowing their slender financial resources, she insisted upon their acceptance of a monthly sum which was more than enough to pay for his board, lodging, and other expenses. Then she moved them into a larger and more comfortable house in a better neighborhood, paying the rent, spending much of the circus "off-season" with them and treating them with a kindness that soon won their hearts. During the "season," the boy frequently traveled with his mother, who had a large private compartment on the circus train, and he had a wonderful time.

This arrangement continued for quite a number of years—my client bringing her son down to see me occasionally—until both of the elderly people died within a few weeks of each other. I was away from Lexington on vacation at that time, and when I got back home the house was closed, and I never saw the mother or her son again.

I recall another episode which is remembered largely, I think, because it resulted in much embarrassment to a prominent and able member of the Lexington police department.

One Saturday afternoon, a white man—quite drunk—staggered down Shreve Avenue, just south of East Main. A colored boy playing a harmonica, or what we used to call a "French harp," sat on the porch of one of the little frame shacks built close to the sidewalk between Main and the C. & O. tracks. The "drunk" reeled up and exclaimed loudly, "Stop that racket, black boy!" Then, as the mouth organ player ignored him, the man grabbed one of the outside window shutters and banged it against the flimsy weather-boarding, repeating his admonition.

At this point the boy got up, went in the house, procured his father's revolver, and returned to the porch. The "drunk," apparently having forgotten the incident, was standing between the sidewalk and the curb, looking up the street. The boy took dead aim and shot his tormentor in the back, just where his suspenders crossed, from which, in the language of the indictment, "he did then and there immediately die."

Since the public mind was still greatly inflamed over the recent tragedy of the Will Lockett mob, the police took no chances and whisked their prisoner off to the penitentiary at Frankfort for safe-keeping. A few days later Judge Kerr called another young lawyer about my age, Harry B. Miller, and me to his office and informed us that the defendant, having no funds with which to employ counsel, would be represented by us on his trial for murder.

This, of course, was a duty no lawyer could evade, so Harry and I set about preparation of our defense as best we could. We visited the little shack on Shreve Avenue and talked to our client's mother. She said he was only fifteen years old, and the vital statistics records corroborated her statement. Meanwhile, court had adjourned for the summer, and although we made several requests of the police department for a date on which we could visit our client at Frankfort we were put off for one reason or another.

However, we were not greatly concerned over this because we had built our whole defense around his extreme youth, about which there could be no dispute. In fact, we thought that the arbitrary action of the police might be turned to our advantage before the jury.

So four months had elapsed before Dudley Veal, Chief of Detectives, called us one morning about seven o'clock and informed us that he had our client in the sheriff's office where we could see him. He also said that the court, mindful of the trouble in the Lockett case, had kept the news from the press but intended to try the defendant that day.

Of course we hurried to the courthouse where, for the first time, we saw our client, sitting handcuffed in the sheriff's outer office—and here we got the shock of our lives! The boy was not only larger and more mature in general appearance than we had expected, but—during the months he had been in prison—he had grown a thick, stubby mustache and a small goatee, which made him look at least thirty years of age!

Concealing our surprise as much as we could, we told officer Veal that we wanted to confer with our client in private, and we took him into the inner office and closed the door. We advised him that his youth was practically the only defense which might save him from the electric chair, on which the prosecution would strongly insist, but that this beard made him look like a full-grown man! It was at this point that the adroit Miller declared, "We've got to get rid of this stuff on his face some way."

"Well," I told him, "I've got a small pocket knife with a fingernail blade just sharpened to a keen edge."

My co-counsel's eyes sparkled, and he replied, "That's what we'll do. You shave him, and I'll furnish the spit!"

Thereupon I undertook the task, while our client groaned and flinched and twisted and rolled his eyes. We found it truly remarkable how a bountiful supply of clear saliva softened tough, wiry hair. It was no fancy job by any means, but it served our purpose reasonably well. Still, we did not think our problem completely solved, because we believed to a certainty that Veal would immediately discover our handiwork; and we braced ourselves stoutly to argue our contention that our client was entitled to appear before the jury looking no older than he actually was. But to our great astonishment and delight, despite his twenty years' experience on the force, Veal saw nothing unusual then or during the trial, at which the jury returned a verdict of life imprisonment, which made the defendant eligible for parole in eight years. When we finally told Veal what had happened, he threw his derby hat to the floor in extreme disgust and self condemnation.

"Ain't I a helluva detective!" he exclaimed. "Why, I couldn't detect a bag of asafetida in a teakettle!" And his associates in the department ribbed him about this as long as he lived.